FOR SALE
WOMEN AND CHILDREN

Trafficking and Forced
Prostitution in Southeast Europe

Igor Davor Gaon • Nancy Forbord

Note for Librarians: A cataloguing record for this book is available from Library and Archives Canada at www.collectionscanada.ca/amicus/index-e.html
ISBN 1-4120-6216-0

*Printed on paper with minimum 30% recycled fibre. Trafford's print shop
runs on "green energy" from solar, wind and other environmentally-friendly power sources.*

PUBLISHING™
Offices in Canada, USA, Ireland and UK
This book was published *on-demand* in cooperation with Trafford Publishing. On-demand publishing is a unique process and service of making a book available for retail sale to the public taking advantage of on-demand manufacturing and Internet marketing. On-demand publishing includes promotions, retail sales, manufacturing, order fulfilment, accounting and collecting royalties on behalf of the author.

Book sales for North America and international:
Trafford Publishing, 6E–2333 Government St.,
Victoria, BC v8t 4p4 CANADA
phone 250 383 6864 (toll-free 1 888 232 4444)
fax 250 383 6804; email to orders@trafford.com
Book sales in Europe:
Trafford Publishing (uk) Ltd., Enterprise House, Wistaston Road Business Centre,
Wistaston Road, Crewe, Cheshire cw2 7rp UNITED KINGDOM
phone 01270 251 396 (local rate 0845 230 9601)
facsimile 01270 254 983; orders.uk@trafford.com
Order online at:
trafford.com/05-1117

10 9 8 7 6 5 4

For Olena
and all victims of human trafficking

Acknowledgements

We very much appreciate the efforts of all those who have helped put this book together. We would first like to thank Maud de Boer-Boquicchio, Deputy Secretary General for the Council of Europe for writing the foreword to this book and for all of her efforts and promotion of activities in the field of migration and human trafficking. We are particularly grateful to Emina Merdan for the many, many hours of translation and other assistance she gave to us. Our thanks also to Suzanne Wertheim, of Northwestern University and Susan Wyle of Stanford University for their help with editing; to Dani Hamilton for her inspiration; to Erika Kayondo for designing the maps and for putting a face on the issue of trafficking in women and children; to Mirza Delibegovic for his steadfastness and patience in getting the copy ready despite many changes; to Leticia Castillo for her creativity in design and layout; and to Melisa Delibegovic and Cardenio Petrucci for their assistance. To Mouvement du Nid of Strasbourg, many thanks for giving us permission to use your photographs and for all your good work in helping women and girls escape the nightmare of trafficking. Finally, thanks to all family and friends who offered support and encouragement in the writing of this book.

Contents

Foreword

In Europe today, we accept the existence of dealers and supermarkets that sell people against their will. You can help yourself from a selection of "cleaners," "sex objects," "beggars," "sundry organs," etc. You can even consult specialized catalogues or agencies which help you to find the person (adult, baby or child), or rather the "object" that you want.

It is happening on our doorsteps, in our industries and our fields, in our embassies and our homes, our fitness centres and our hotels. All kinds of customers use the services that are offered: sick people, executives, diplomats, lonely men. Against all logic, our society seems to tolerate this new form of slavery.

Trafficking in human beings is patently a crime. And this crime generates other crimes. Its illicit profits are frequently used for corruption and other criminal activities. It is therefore urgent that the criminals are prosecuted and that preventive measures are taken to avoid it spreading any further.

But trafficking in human beings is above all an affront to human dignity. As victims of violations of their fundamental rights, trafficked persons are entitled to adequate protection, from a physical, material, psychological and legal point of view.

By its very nature trafficking nearly always involves several states. To address the question effectively, international co-operation is a must. The international community feels concerned and this is excellent news. Many initiatives have been taken to fight trafficking. The Council of Europe has elaborated recommendations and action plans (both at international and national levels), reviewed national legislations, implemented assistance programmes, launched awareness raising campaigns and monitored progress. But there remains much to be done.

Trafficking in human beings is a global scourge. All member states of the Council of Europe are concerned. All of them have ratified the European Convention on Human Rights and have committed themselves to numerous other international texts which prohibit slavery, torture and inhuman or degrading treatment. It is thus only natural that they are determined today to fight trafficking by means of a legally binding instrument: the Council of Europe Convention on Action Against Trafficking in Human Beings. This Convention is based on the three "Pillars": Prevention, Prosecution, and last, but not least, Protection of the victims.

International action has little chance to obtain results without the commitment of national and local governments, law enforcement authorities, the business sector, the media and civil society as a whole. The authors of this book prove that victims are closer to us than we realize. We should therefore feel concerned by their destiny. After explaining the complexity of trafficking, they describe the many initiatives that can be undertaken to effectively fight it. Their personal commitment to the cause of combating trafficking is a shining example of all that we can accomplish on an individual level.

I therefore invite you to discover the dramatic stories behind these pages, to follow the authors' reasoning and to believe in their message of hope. I encourage you to identify what you can do. And I urge you to do it. Don't wait.

Maud de Boer-Buquicchio
Deputy Secretary General
Council of Europe

PART I

An Overview of Trafficking in Southeast Europe

The Life and Death of Olena, Trafficking Victim

In November 2004, Olena, a young woman from Ukraine, died of AIDS in a hospital in Mostar, Bosnia and Herzegovina. She was 21 years old and a victim of trafficking. Olena also suffered from chronic syphilis, tuberculosis and hepatitis C. When she was a teenager, she was kidnapped by pimps and forced into prostitution. She never chose this profession.

Prior to bringing her to Bosnia and Herzegovina, the people who kidnapped Olena took her first to Slovenia and then to Serbia. During the last year of her life, she was confined by her pimps to an apartment in Mostar, where she was forced to provide sexual services to clients. One newspaper reported that even young boys from Mostar's schools came in groups to gain sexual experience in the apartment where she was held.

She was also rented out to individuals and groups. At the end of September, Olena was presented as a 21st birthday gift to a young man in the small town of Citluk near Mostar. She had been "rented" by a friend of her pimp's for this occasion. According to the testimony of one man at the party, Olena had unprotected sex with five young men. "We were drunk and I didn't plan to have sex with her, but it happened to me, and that's it."

The shocking news and publicity surrounding her death from AIDS caused panic among her former pimps, clients, and many others from the region. It is reported that in the last few months of her life in Mostar, she had sexual relations with as many as 1,000 men. There is no way to know for sure just how many persons have been infected with AIDS, syphilis, tuberculosis and hepatitis C as a result of contact with Olena, her pimps, or her clients.

The death of Olena has opened a new discussion in Bosnia and Herzegovina about the extent of trafficking in women and children. Previously, authorities had maintained that with the crackdown on prostitution in night clubs and bars, trafficking for purposes of sexual exploitation no longer existed in the country.

The head of Mostar's La Strada, an organization which assists women and children who are victims of trafficking, said it was a shame that a young girl had to die before the authorities understood that trafficking is one of biggest problems facing Bosnia and Herzegovina. She also said that journalists were incorrectly calling Olena a prostitute rather than a victim of trafficking, which she was.

Reports on Olena's death appeared in Bosnia and Herzegovina's newspapers "Oslobodjene" and "Dnevni Avaz" on November 8, 2004.

Introduction

"'Trafficking in persons' shall mean the recruitment, transportation, transfer, harbouring or receipt of persons, by means of the threat or use of force or other forms of coercion, of abduction, of fraud, of deception, of the abuse of power or of a position of vulnerability or of the giving or receiving of payments or benefits to achieve the consent of a person having control over another person, for the purpose of exploitation. Exploitation shall include, at a minimum, the exploitation of the prostitution of others or other forms of sexual exploitation, forced labor or services, slavery or practices similar to slavery, servitude or the removal of organs."

United Nations Protocol to Prevent, Suppress, and Punish Trafficking in Persons Especially Women and Children, December 2000

Every year hundreds of thousands of men, women, and children around the world are captured and enslaved by organized crime in the horrendous enterprise known as "human trafficking." Organized crime ensnares the poor, the weak, the young, the old, and migrants fleeing conflict and civil disruption, and, in the process, deprives these people of their human rights, their dignity, and their hopes of a better life. Just as with other enterprises in which it is involved such as trafficking in drugs, weapons, and other black market commodities, organized crime often enlists sophisticated resources and techniques to enable it to control the market in human beings. The selling and exploitation of people who are forced into conditions of slavery and used as cheap labor or sexual objects is surely the darkest side of organized crime.[1]

Human trafficking is now the third-biggest activity of organized crime in Europe, surpassed only by trafficking in drugs and arms.[2] No doubt human trafficking would exist without organized crime, but not at such a high level. In fact, one of the reasons so many women and children[3] are ensnared and sold into sexual slavery is because the networks used for human trafficking were already in place within several types of criminal organizations. So there is a strong connection between drug trafficking and human trafficking[4] – very often the same routes, the same people, and the same organizations are used for trafficking of both drugs and people.[5] The fight against human trafficking is therefore a simultaneous attack on drug trafficking.

The business of trafficking in human beings is flourishing as people are bought and sold to work in sweatshops, as beggars and thieves, and in prostitution and pornography. As shocking as it may seem, even babies and small children, who have been abducted outright or sold by parents or relatives are victims of this barbaric commerce.[6] Human trafficking is highly lucrative. It is estimated that the buying and selling of human beings worldwide generates as much as seven billion US dollars in income per year.[7]

Most people, including government officials, simply do not recognize the seriousness of the phenomenon of human trafficking. It is really no less than 21st Century slavery. Although we tend to think of slavery as belonging to bygone eras, it is happening right now in the most civilized and modern capitals of the world. In Europe, people are being bought and sold, held against their will, and required to perform work under the most degrading conditions. They are stripped of their documents and sometimes their identities, threatened, raped, and often tortured. And for most of these victims, there is little recourse as they are deprived of friends, family, and legal systems that could assist them to safety. All of this is happening in the heart of the European Union and across the Atlantic in the United States.

One of the problems with the international fight against trafficking in human beings is that there is no single agreed-upon definition of trafficking in human beings. Many confuse it with "voluntary" prostitution or smuggling. But, although the distinctions are often difficult to grasp, trafficking is distinct. Those who are trafficked lose their ability to control their destinies as they are enslaved or bonded into service. They are not working to put food on their own tables, but to enrich the coffers of the traffickers who hold them captive, abuse them, and control their lives. Even women who have decided to work in the sex industry abroad because they are in a desperate economic situation do not expect the miserable, violent, dangerous enslavement that they will find themselves in once they are lured into the hands of traffickers. Their fate often involves force, violence, rape, abuse, exposure to illness, and torture. Some victims of human trafficking are murdered by traffickers; others end up committing suicide.

Men, women, and children may all be victims of trafficking, but the fact is that the majority are women and children who are bought and sold for sexual exploitation.[8] In Europe and the United States, the demand for paid sex has fueled the trafficking of women and children from Eastern and

Southeastern Europe. Within Southeastern Europe itself, there has been a ready and aggressive market for sex services with the large presence of international soldiers and international workers.

The realities of the post-conflict and economic situations in the region have led to mass migration of women and girls seeking a better life. The situation for many of these people is like a ball in a pinball machine; they are pushed and pulled by forces beyond their control. These forces could be economic or social or political in nature, pushing them out of one country and pulling them towards another. But, faced with strict immigration policies of Western countries, they seek out other ways of getting to the "promised land" making them especially vulnerable to traffickers who lure them with promises of actual jobs with real pay. In some cases the traffickers simply abduct women and children or buy them from parents or relatives who are in dire financial straits. Sometimes these families actually believe that their trafficked family members will send money back home from abroad.

Of the approximately 700,000 women and children around the world who become victims of some kind of human trafficking each year,[9] it is estimated that 200,000 of them pass through the Balkans.[10] Southeastern Europe has thus become a major center for trafficking in women and children for prostitution. Organized crime has gained a strong foothold in the region and is viciously exploiting the most vulnerable element of the population. The women and children of Southeast Europe are for sale, and human traffickers are buying and selling them like chattel for enormous profits.

Governments have not dealt effectively with this problem, and, in fact, the issue is not a priority for most countries. Many consider human trafficking a problem of "illegal" or "irregular" migration rather than a criminal problem and treat trafficked people as criminals rather than the victims they are. There is a lack of harmonization in the criminal laws of the states, making it very difficult to combat organized crime. Police and border guards are often complicit, assisting the traffickers and getting paid for it. There is also corruption at the highest levels: prosecutors, judges, government officials, high ranking politicians, and international workers have been accused of being involved in trafficking.[11] Rather than giving victims the opportunity to testify and give crucial information regarding the traffickers which could lead to their prosecution, the victims are usually swiftly returned to their home countries as undocumented migrants into the very same conditions from which they left.

Much work must be done by individuals, governments, and the international community if this problem is going to be solved, and it will require financial support. Public awareness, international cooperation, national legislation, training of law enforcement officials, and local action will all have to be mobilized to a much greater and more committed extent if women and children are to be protected from the scourge of trafficking.

Notes:

1. Organized crime is a worldwide phenomenon that has been described as a criminal network better organized and spreading faster internationally than any legal business. Each country has its own definition of organized crime and in accordance with its legislation, deals with these illegal operations within the frame of its own criminal code. Unfortunately, as world globalization spreads, the number of enterprises that are open to all kinds of cooperation, but also to organized crime, also increases.

Because of its excellent organization, organized crime is spreading rapidly, and has easily recognizable international dimensions. It is difficult for a state, acting on its own, to fight this kind of crime, so that tackling the problem requires both a regional and global approach. This can be accomplished through collecting and processing information and classifying and exchanging that information, which requires international cooperation in open combat against this phenomenon which must include harmonization of legislation.

Many factors influence how criminal enterprises organize and operate and the phenomenon varies from the state to the international level, but there is no doubt that the rapid technological revolution over the last ten years has provided excellent equipment and a sophisticated approach that has allowed international crime to flourish. Thanks to modern technology organized crime is well connected, and with the loosening of state borders new opportunities for easy movement have emerged which give criminal elements new possibilities and, thereby, decrease the ability of those charged to combat and prevent it. The European Commission, in its report "A Union Policy Against Corruption," dated May 1997, underlined that the creation of a uniform market at the European Union level and the signing of the Schengen Agreement would cause a virtual abolition of and higher vulnerability of border control.

2. Igor Davor Gaon, *Trafficking in Human Beings. Reflection Tables on Immigration and Human Rights,* (Athens, Council of Europe – Office of the Commissioner for Human Rights in cooperation with Marangopoulos Foundation for Human Rights, 5 April 2003).

3. The term "children" in this book refers to those people under the age of eighteen who, under the Convention on the Rights of the Child, are children.

4. According to the U.S. Drug Enforcement Agency.

5. For example: boats that bring trafficked women from Albania to Italy return carrying cigarettes.

6. "UNICEF Report on Child Prostitution on the Czech-German Border," *Deutsche Welle* 2003 <http://www.dw-world.de>.

7. J. Widgren, "International Response to Trafficking in Migrants and the Safeguarding of Migrant Rights," paper presented on the 11th IOM Seminar on Migration, Geneva, 1994.

8. There is little data on the trafficking of men into Western Europe. The experience is different in the United States, where men are identified as victims of trafficking and forced labor. <www.cia.gov/csi/monograph/women/trafficking.pdf>.

9. See <http://europa.eu.int/comm/employment_social/equ_opp/index_en.htm>.

10. According to the US Drug Enforcement Agency (DEA), 200,000 victims of trafficking pass through the Balkan region.

11. *Mina News Agency,* Podgorica, Montenegro, May 2003.

Chapter 1

How Women and Children Become Ensnared in Sexual Slavery

"Tatyana," a 19 year old Ukrainian, responded to an advertisement in a Kiev newspaper for a job in a beauty salon in Germany. With a fake passport she traveled to Frankfurt where she was told that the job had already been given to someone else, and that she would have to go to Belgium to work in the same chain of beauty salons. When she finally arrived in Belgium, she was told that she now owed her trafficker 10,000 € and would have to pay it back by working as a prostitute. She managed to escape and went to the police, but they arrested her because she had no legal documents.

Interview with "Tatyana," Kiev, Ukraine 2003

Southeast Europe is a prime location for the three different stages of human trafficking: it is a region of origin, transit, and destination. In this chapter, we will focus on Southeast Europe as a region of origin, and the ways that women and girls from the countries and regions of Southeast Europe are ensnared and recruited by traffickers. Women and girls are taken from Albania, Bulgaria, Macedonia, Moldova, Serbia, Montenegro, Kosovo, Romania, and Ukraine. The trafficked women and girls end up in Western Europe, Scandinavia, Turkey, the Near East, Asia, and North America. Here is how:

Most often, victims of trafficking are people who have made the decision to leave their country and look for work abroad. They are usually poor, in difficult financial circumstances, and think that work abroad, even if obtained through illegal channels, is the only way to better their situation. There are several ways that traffickers make contact with their victims:

- The victim reads a newspaper ad offering a well-paid job in Western Europe. The person who has placed the ad is a trafficker, and, instead of assisting with migration and employment, will funnel the woman into the system of trafficking.

- Someone whom the victim already knows, often a woman or even a member of the victim's family, offers her an attractive job in Western Europe – again, instead of assisting with employment, this contact person places the victim into the hands of traffickers.

- Victims are approached by a trafficker directly, someone who claims to have contacts for good jobs in Western Europe.

- Victims are simply abducted by traffickers.

- Traffickers or their recruiters contact women who are already working in the sex industry and suggest that the women move abroad to find more lucrative work. Instead, the women end up in conditions of sexual slavery, with working and living conditions far worse than those they were promised.

• Family members, neighbours, or acquaintances arrange marriages with men living abroad. However, instead of getting married, once they leave the country, the woman and girls end up in the hands of traffickers.

Who are the traffickers involved in the recruiting and subsequent exploitation of these women? Because of the huge profits, criminal organizations from many different regions take part in ensnaring women and girls in Southeast Europe. They include: Albanian criminal organizations, Balkan regional mafias, Eastern European criminal organizations, and Western European criminal organizations. Turkish,[1] Bulgarian,[2] Ukrainian,[3] and Russian[4] criminal groups are also involved. However, Albanian criminal groups are the dominant players in human trafficking in Southeast Europe. It has been estimated that they control more than 60% of Balkan trafficking, using the same routes for humans and for drugs, and they also control street prostitution in several cities in Western Europe.[5]

How do traffickers trap a recruited woman? Most often she is tricked into turning over her passport to the trafficker, who will tell her that it is being taken for a visa stamp – the trafficker will pretend to be facilitating her passage to the country of destination. Passports themselves are valuable, since once they are falsified; they can be used for the transport of multiple trafficked women.

Once the ensnared women are without documents, they become vulnerable. Realizing they are in a precarious position, they are more likely to cooperate. This lack of valid documentation also keeps them from going to the police in the destination country. Their exploiters (traffickers, or owners of

Passport of a Trafficked Woman

brothels, nightclubs, or bars) tell them that they have no legal status and no right to live or work in the country, and that they will end up in jail if they go to the police or have any contact with them.

Once they have been ensnared, had their documentation stolen, and been smuggled across national borders, the women are sold to pimps, brothel owners, bar, and nightclub owners, all of whom can be considered slave owners. The women's living and working conditions are nightmarish and their human rights are violated in many ways:

- They have no control over their lives or their work, and are completely at the mercy of their exploiters. Their exploiters decide everything: what sexual services they will provide, how many days a week, and to how many men. They control what they wear, what they eat, and their access to medical care.[6]

- They are forced to have unprotected sex with multiple clients; this makes them vulnerable to unwanted pregnancy and to sexually transmitted diseases, including HIV/AIDS.

- Sometimes they are forced by their exploiters to become drug addicts; this makes them easier to control.

- They are sold, resold, and transported without any choice or control on their part – 50% of the women and girls who are forced into sexual slavery change owners, places of residence, and sometimes even their country of residence.

- They are subjected to both physical and psychological abuse. They are raped by their exploiters, and beaten if they show resistance (and sometimes even if they don't). The exploiters may also use psychological blackmail. Traffickers in Western Europe often have ties to organized crime in the victims' countries of origin, so they can easily blackmail them by threatening to harm their families if they do not cooperate.

- They end up in a foreign country where they probably do not speak the language, are isolated, do not have contacts, and do not have a support system. They do not know where to go for help, and do not even know how to ask for help.

- Even if they ask for help, the local police are sometimes in collusion with traffickers, and instead of helping the victims and referring them to organizations that provide assistance, they return the victims to the slaveholders.

Victims end up hopeless and in despair, infected with venereal diseases, underfed, and ill. They can be arrested and treated as criminals. They are denied medical care, legal aid, and restitution, and are seen as a burden to the judicial system, which usually treats them as illegal aliens and not as victims of organized crime. They then become double victims: victimized first by traffickers, and then victimized by countries that criminalize them. Many victims are deported back to their home countries, where they face all the same problems that drove them to leave in the first place, with the additional burdens of mental and physical trauma, social stigma, and ostracism. Finally, some victims end up dead – either murdered by their exploiters when they become too problematic or are no longer useful, or as the result of suicide.

Here is the story of one victim of trafficking – we will call her Dana.[7]

> *Dana grew up in a small town in Moldova, where she lived with her parents. Even though she had a good education, including two years of university, she couldn't find decent work in her hometown, or in the nation's capital, Chisinau. Dana watched American and European movies and television programs and saw how there was better work and a higher standard of living in the West. She decided that she needed to leave Moldova in order to find work so that she could make enough money to support her family that was falling deeper and deeper into poverty.*
>
> *One day, Dana was talking with her friend about moving to Western Europe to find work. The friend had seen an ad in the newspaper about restaurant jobs in Italy, and passed the contact information along. Dana met with a man who had placed the ad, and he told her that not only could he arrange for a job in a restaurant in Italy, but that he would take care of all of the details of immigration, including the paperwork.*
>
> *The day that Dana left Moldova, this man had her fill out job and visa applications,*

and made sure that she had her passport with her. They drove to the Romanian border, where she was dropped off to wait for the man's associate while he went around picking up other prospective employees. The man reassured her that his associate would take care of the border crossing, and that they would meet up again in Romania.

At the Romanian border, the associate took Dana's passport and paperwork and conferred with the border guards at length. Finally, they were waved through. By then it was late at night, and they drove through darkness until they reached a nightclub. The associate delivered her to the nightclub's owner, and drove away. The situation seemed strange, so Dana checked her paperwork to make sure everything was in order. But she saw immediately that her passport was missing. At that moment she realized she was in trouble – but she had no idea how bad the situation would be.

Dana pleaded with the nightclub owner to help her – but instead of helping her, he threatened to beat her, especially if she didn't do exactly what he said. Then her nightmare began. The nightclub owner locked her into a small room at the back of the club and left her there, returned later and then raped her. Dana was completely at his mercy: he controlled her every move. She frantically tried to find a way to escape, but there was no way out.

After several days of being locked in the back room, beaten, starved, and raped repeatedly by the nightclub owner, Dana was picked up by a new man who drove her to Serbia. He also threatened to punish her brutally if she didn't follow his instructions, and eventually delivered her to an apartment in Belgrade where she was held prisoner with several other women who had fallen into the same trap. The man who was in charge of the apartment brought Dana and another woman to a Belgrade slave market where they were purchased by an Albanian man and smuggled into Albania. In Albania, Dana was once again sold at a slave market, and ended up being smuggled into Italy where she was forced by her Albanian owner to work as a prostitute in a brothel. She was now in Italy, her original destination, but in conditions more horrible than she ever could have imagined.

By the time Dana arrived in Italy, she was in terrible shape mentally and emotionally. She had spent much of her life protecting her virtue and reputation, and had already been nervous about leaving her home to go work abroad. Then she had suddenly been thrust into a nightmare: repeatedly raped and beaten, threatened with further punishment, suddenly under the control of men who cared nothing for her except for the amount of money she could earn for them. She didn't speak Italian beyond the few words she had learned in preparation for her trip.

Dana's pimp put her to work on the streets and controlled her every move. After a few weeks, he handed her over to another pimp and disappeared. While she was working for the second pimp, handing over all her money to him each morning and then being locked into an apartment with other trafficked women, she was picked up on the streets by the police and arrested for prostitution. She was unable to show that she was in the country legally and so was given a 15-day deportation notice. Her pimp then sold her to yet another pimp, and a few days later she was arrested once more on charges of prostitution. This time the police kept her in custody, and then, after it was confirmed that she was Moldovan, they arranged for her to be deported.

After Dana's arrest, her parents were informed that she had been working as a prostitute in Italy and had been deported because she did not have proper authorization to be in the country. Soon, word of her arrest for prostitution and deportation spread through the community, and she was the primary subject of gossip for weeks. Pressure from neighbours and other family members convinced Dana's parents that she would be a black mark not only on the family, but on the community as well. They arranged for a family friend to meet Dana on her way back to her hometown and instead to take her to the home of a distant relative in a village located in a different region.

Now Dana has been back in Moldova for a year. She is living in exile from her family and friends, from her home and community. She still has the same problems finding work as before, but her situation is much worse than it was before she left: she is still traumatized from her terrible experiences, and her chances of finding a Moldovan husband are now almost nil. Dana has no idea why or how she fell into the situation that she did, and has no sense that she was the victim of an organized system of human trafficking – this is because no one has treated her like a victim.

Instead, they have treated her like a prostitute, a criminal, and a fallen woman.

Dana is thinking about again leaving Moldova and once more looking for work in Western Europe. She thinks that she was just the victim of terrible luck, and that if she is more careful this time, things will turn out better.

Notes:

1. T. Cretin, *Mafias du monde,* (Paris: Presses Universitaires de France, 2002) 67-68.
2. *Le Nouvel Observateur*, août 2002: 20-28.
3. *Messages*, avril 2003 and *Washington Times*, 13 March 2001.
4. *Agence France Presse*, 12 February 1998. See:<http://www.antislavery. org/homepage/antislavery/traffickingrussia.htm>.
5. *The Guardian,* 26 March 2003. See: <www.guardian.co.uk/comment/ story/0,3604,921977,00.html>.
6. Medical care is charged to the victim, and considered part of the "debt" the trafficked victim must work off for the exploiter who purchased her.
7. Dana is not her real name. In order to protect the identity of this person some of the details of her ordeal are combined with stories from other trafficking victims.

Chapter 2

Who is Responsible for Human Trafficking?

One woman from Moldova, interviewed by Human Rights Watch during her stay at the IOM shelter in Sarajevo in April 2001, reported that she was bought and sold by traffickers four times. Trafficked to Bosnia and Herzegovina in July 2000, she told of traveling by taxi, bus, and boat, in car trunks, and on foot before finally reaching the establishment owned by the man who had purchased her for 1,026 €.

"Hopes Betrayed" – Report on Human Trafficking in Bosnia and Herzegovina, Human Rights Watch 2002

As Dana's story illustrates, no single individual, criminal group, system or government is uniquely responsible for human trafficking. Certain people and groups, in particular organized crime, are clearly more responsible for trafficking and forced prostitution than others. But, in fact, many different individuals, groups, and conditions contribute to the problem of trafficking, either by creating systems and situations where human trafficking is both possible and profitable, by directly engaging in trafficking activities, or by purchasing the sex services of trafficking victims.

Both human trafficking and organized crime in Southeast Europe have been described as having weak, almost non-existent organization and hierarchy. This characterization gives the wrong impression that the people involved are just loosely associated with one another, or have only loose connections with organized crime. However, the connections are often stronger than are immediately obvious. This wrong impression can make it difficult to recognize the patterns and systems of human trafficking – even victims themselves sometimes do not realize that their situation is the end result of human trafficking.

Through Dana's story it is easy to see how this could

happen. Many different people played a role in her victimization and exploitation - some of those involved played a very small role – it was the chain of individuals and events that ensnared her. So, even Dana herself does not realize that she was captured and exploited by an established trafficking system.

Here is how the people Dana encountered on the way played a part in her descent into sexual slavery, and how their activities contribute to the problem of human trafficking in Southeast Europe. Although this story illustrates what happened to a single victim, the people described here are typical of those who might be involved in the chain of trafficking.

- The man who placed the advertisement about the restaurant job in Italy - this man earns money by supplying a passport thief near the border of Romania with both young women and their passports. He therefore knows that the women will end up having their passports stolen. He justifies his actions because the money he gains helps support his family. People like this can work alone, in connection with corrupted authorities, or as part of an organized criminal network. He supplied Dana with her passport, which may have been original or may have been falsified. A single passport may be used for several victims.

- The passport thief - this person has an excellent link with the one who placed the ad about the restaurant job in Italy. He does more than just steal passports. He has a deal with a night club owner in Romania to deliver young women to him, and gets a nice sum of money for each woman he delivers. Since he has a heroin habit, the night club owner also supplies him with heroin. Sometimes he forces the women to have sex with him before he turns them over to the club owner.

- The border officials - these people are paid so little for their work that they rely on bribes paid to them by various types of smugglers in order to supplement their incomes. They take bribes in order to be able to put food on the table. From their point of view, they have no problem helping young women from Moldova to go abroad to find work, but at the same time they are aware that these women might end up in forced prostitution.[1]

- The night club owner - this man makes extra money by being a "transit point" for women and for drugs. He delivers the women to organized crime groups and also distributes the drugs that he gets from them.

- The driver to Serbia - he is from Romania, but many such drivers are from Serbia. He is part of a network of traffickers and is involved in several different "jobs." On behalf of his "employer," this man pays the owner of the nightclub a "holding fee" for the women held hostage in the club and then smuggles them into Serbia where they are sold in a slave market.

- The Belgrade man who imprisons and sells women - he is also a part of organized crime and belongs to one of the clans from Belgrade (the Zemun, Surcin, and Zvezdar clans).

- The man who buys Dana in Belgrade - this man is part of an organized crime group. He thinks of his job as "harvesting a crop" in Serbia and selling it on the Albanian marketplace. It doesn't make much of a difference to him that the "crop" is human. The criminal group with which he is loosely associated gives him "protection" and contacts, and in exchange, he gives them a percentage of his profit.

- The gang "Boss" - the head of the organized criminal group wasn't mentioned in Dana's story because she never encountered him. He has no contact with the women whose enslavement brings him such great profit. He thinks of his business as a franchise, and has "traders" located throughout Southeast Europe – they provide him with a steady stream of profit, and his personal level of risk is minimal.

- The man who buys Dana in Albania - this man traffics women from Albania into Italy on a standard smuggling route on the Adriatic. In Italy he resells the women he purchased to pimps working in Italy (many of them Albanians) and then loads up his boats with cigarettes, which he sells upon his return to Albania.

- Dana's pimp in Italy - he is a member of the same clan as the man who bought Dana. This clan is part of an efficiently organized network that rarely makes a mistake.[2]

The actions and illegal activities of the people who took part in Dana's story are exploited by organized crime and used to turn women into commodities and slaves. In addition, their activities take place against the backdrop of two systems that help continue the human trafficking process: the black market, and the black market in labor.

THE BLACK MARKET

The black market has been an integral part of the economy of Southeast Europe for more than three generations. During communist times, the black market was perceived as a benign force, an unofficial system that allowed people to obtain goods or services that were either unavailable or highly regulated by the communist government. Since the region's transition to a free market economy, this system has continued to operate. Where there is a need, people will find a way to supply it, and this is how a black market emerges. The people who engage in black market activity in Southeast Europe are not necessarily villains or evil; they are often people simply seizing an opportunity to provide for themselves and their families. But whenever money and goods are exchanged outside of the legitimate economy, there is the potential for blackmail, extortion, and human exploitation. It is in this way that the black market has contributed to the problem of human trafficking in Southeast Europe.

Since the black market operates outside of government restrictions and is able to evade government enforcement, it is a system that is ripe for use by organized crime. Criminal organizations take advantage of opportunities made available through black market habits and systems, and thus introduced human trafficking and drug trafficking into the black market economy – these activities are risky but extremely profitable. Although black market activity can be found almost everywhere to a certain degree, a thriving black market is usually a sign that a country has social, political or economic instability. Countries that have effective governments and developed economies have less black market activity than countries with transitional or unstable governments and economies.

In the case of Southeast Europe, the black market has flourished as governments still struggle for legitimacy, economies are weak, and the rule of law is shaky. Organized crime has not missed the opportunity to insert itself into this system with trafficking in all areas including human beings.

THE BLACK MARKET OF LABOR

The imbalance between transitional countries and their more stable neighbours has created a system of supply and demand for human labor. In stable, wealthy countries, there is a demand for cheap labor to do manual, low-prestige, or "dirty" work for little pay. In transitional countries with unstable economies, widespread poverty, and little local economic opportunity for betterment, there are a significant number of people who have reached such a point of despair that they are willing to put themselves at risk and move to another country where they can find a job and maybe make enough money to send some home to help support their families. These people thus become the supply to meet the demands for cheap labor in the wealthier countries.

When stable countries have liberal immigration laws, easy access to temporary work permits, legitimate jobs, and social services available to immigrants, there is very little need or demand for a black market in labor. However, when the countries that have the need for cheap labor also have stringent immigration laws and act to repel potential immigrants, allow the jobs they fill to remain outside the system of legal employment, and deny them social services, there is a situation ripe for exploitation by a black market in labor. The smuggling of human beings becomes profitable, because people are willing to pay for someone to organize the way and means to get them to a place where they can have a decent paying job. Once these systems of illegal immigration are in place, it is easy for traffickers to exploit these systems – and it becomes difficult for a migrant to tell the difference between a smuggler and a trafficker.

Because of economic and social instability, widespread poverty, and a poor job market in which women are the last to be hired and the first to lose jobs, Southeast Europe has become a major source of illegal and exploited female migrants to the West. There are also other important factors that contribute to trafficking in women and children.

THE CUSTOMER

Without a market for services provided by sex workers, there would, of course, be no trafficking in human beings for sexual exploitation. It is the demands of the market and the needs of male customers or clients that fuels the existence of trafficking in women and children. Clients of the sex trade therefore play the vital role in trafficking, as traffickers will do everything possible to satisfy their demand and thus keep themselves in business.

Yet very little is written about the culpability of the customer in promoting sexual slavery. And, in many cases, laws and penalties are mild or non-existent against the customer, sometimes even in cases involving children.

Few studies have actually been done regarding the role of customers in human trafficking or about men who buy sex from prostitutes. One of the likely reasons for this is because the men seek anonymity and are not eager in any way to draw attention to themselves. The question of the client has also been generally ignored in public debates and legislation concerning prostitution.[2]

Author Louise Brown notes this research gap in her book *Sex Slaves*. She states, "Some magical things happen in the sex industry. One of the most remarkable tricks is just how often the customers vanish from both analysis and censure...Only a few of the many reports written on the trafficking of women and prostitution pay any attention to who is buying sex as opposed to who is selling it."[3] In fact, from reading most of the available reports, statements, and legal documents relating to trafficking in human beings, one could easily be led to believe that the sex trade involves only poor women and organized crime.[4]

So who are the clients and why do they seek the services of sex workers? The few studies that have been done cite a variety of clientele and reasons for their seeking paid sex. The clients are tourists, soldiers, men working abroad, and local residents. Some research suggests that the increase of male demand for paid sex is logical in the sense that it is more available - "privileges" formerly restricted by class, race and gender, are now available to everybody; in other words, it is not necessary to be rich in order to hire a prostitute.[5] Perhaps this increased availability has whetted the demand for more paid sex. It might also be that Southeast Europe, Eastern Europe, and Russia have produced a pool of well educated young women who enter prostitution either by choice or through sexual slavery, and this type of woman appeals to many men who might not otherwise have been willing to pay for sex.

There are other theories about what drives the clients. Some suggest it is due to changes in Western culture in which increasing numbers of men live alone. Many men are not integrated into the local community and have few personal relationships – they are isolated and lonely. This, combined with the fact that many people work long hours and have little time for social life, has lead to an increasing demand for the relaxation and interactions offered by massage parlors, dancing bars, brothels, street prostitution, and sex tourism. For some men, only prostitutes provide moments of recognition or satisfaction and they find that sex is available only if they buy it.[6]

More researchers need to ask questions of clients such as what they know about trafficking, if they would buy the sexual services of a person held in sexual bondage, and why they seek out prostitutes. There is an astonishing lack of information about the consumers of paid sex – those who have created the demand that drives trafficking.

GLOBALIZATION

Globalization, so called post-contemporary society, has created a new form of international relations characterized by the erosion of state power, the growth of multinational institutions and companies, and an international market with fewer borders. Globalization has resulted in the expansion of various types of exchanges and movement: the exchange of information, the expansion of tourism, and an increase in migration across borders that have, with the weakening of the state, become more porous. Part of this increase is related to prostitution, as the demand for sex workers has increased. Organized crime took immediate advantage of the opportunities created by the increased demand for paid sex found in globalized Europe, and has filled this demand through various methods of exploitation, including human trafficking and sexual slavery.

Many blame globalization for the weakening of social relations and local culture, including working class culture, gender culture, and neighborhood culture and what we call "common values of the traditional family." Economic pressures have led to community instability and family breakdown. With jobs unavailable at home, people look elsewhere for work and many look abroad for hope. This is leading to a disappearance of the common culture of communities and relationships within communities. Many cultural taboos, such as those against prostitution, have withered and in many cases community standards have lapsed. With these tears in the fabric of society, especially in Southeast Europe, women have often been thrust into the role of decision makers with the responsibility to provide for the future of the family. Consequently, they are faced with the painful and complex possibility of looking abroad to find work thus making them vulnerable to traffickers.

THE INTERNATIONAL PRESENCE

There is little doubt that the large number of international soldiers and employees of international organizations has fueled the demand for paid sex in Southeast Europe which has contributed to the trafficking epidemic particularly in Bosnia and Herzegovina, Kosovo, and Macedonia. Local NGOs believe that the presence of thousands of expatriate civilians and soldiers has been a significant motivating factor for traffickers to Bosnia and Herzegovina.[7] As conflict enveloped the Balkans in the early 1990s, international troops and aid workers moved into the region. In Bosnia and Herzegovina more than 60,000 international soldiers and aid workers took up residence immediately following the conflict. Most were men without families. Organized crime immediately recognized the opportunity for prostitution and in a short time trafficking in women and girls exploded on the scene. In Kosovo and Macedonia the scenario has been similar. But the single factor most responsible for the growth in human trafficking is organized crime, and we will look at that in the next chapter.

«If you discovered a trafficked woman, what would you do?»

Respondent from Banja Luka (Bosnia and Herzegovina):

When I think about it, I would not know who to turn to, because those whose job is to defend law and order, they are the main protagonists or an important "supportive" factor. So, I am lost now. A poor person, in the middle of all this corruption, does not dare to report a minor crime, not to mention something related to prostitution and trafficking, because we all know how strong are the "brothers" who are the "bosses" in our town in this business and who keep people, and to them beating me is like to you saying "Good afternoon."

From Research on Trafficking in Bosnia and Herzegovina by UNICEF and Save the Children Norway, 2005

Notes:

1. Apparently corruption of border guards is the rule rather than the exception – see Barbara Limanowska, *Trafficking in Human Beings in Southeastern Europe* (Belgrade: UNICEF, UNOHCHR, OSCE/ODIHR, 2002) 9.
2. In Recommendation No. R (2000), 11 the drafters wished to encourage governments to initiate research in this direction. See Council of Europe Committee of Ministers' Recommendation No. R (2000) 11, pg. 21.
3. Louise Brown, *Sex Slaves, The Trafficking of Women in Asia* (London: Virago Press, 2001) 129.
4. Ibid.
5. Susanne Thorbek, "Prostitution in a Global Context: Changing Patterns," *Transnational Prostitution*, ed. Susanne Thorbeck and Bandana Pattanaik (London: Zed Books Ltd, 2002) 2.
6. Thorbek 38.
7. *Hopes Betrayed*, Human Rights Watch, Vol. 14, No. 9 (D), 2002: 11.

Chapter 3

The Role of
Organized Crime

The problem should be tackled within the context of organized crime. It is certainly downplayed at the moment. The police force needs additional training to better understand the problem and a clear break from the sweeping-it-under-the-rug policy. Still, I have serious doubts that we can eliminate it completely. (A high-ranking police officer in Croatia).

From "Trafficking In Women and Children For Sexual Exploitation" IOM, Zagreb 2002

Human trafficking in Europe is inextricably linked to organized crime. The fight against trafficking must take into account measures against organized crime. The rise of organized crime in Southeast Europe is one of the region's biggest problems, and is directly connected to the last decade's difficult move from state-based to market-based economies, and from regional and ethnic conflict to reconstruction.

International conferences[1] and studies have noted that countries in transition are particularly vulnerable to organized crime, and that the activities of criminal organizations can develop more quickly and become stronger than the legal economy of these countries. Criminal organizations generate sources of income through the operation of black-market exchanges, including the sale of cigarettes, alcohol, and other luxury items. Then, supported by this black market income, organized crime gains power and subverts the country's economy and tax collection. This undermines a healthy transition to the new economy: people have no confidence in their politicians because the government lacks the funds to provide necessary social services such as retirement funds, health insurance, and infrastructure improvements. Additional problems include police forces that are more easily susceptible to corruption due to extremely low salaries and judicial systems that are still limited in power, with the end result of weak police enforcement and the inability of a government to ensure the rule of law.

Countries define organized crime differently according to their legislation, and they prosecute criminal organizations within their own criminal code. However, a general definition would include:

- organized crime involves at least two people, but almost always more;
- organized crime has as its aim the acquisition of power and profit;
- organized crime uses violence or intimidation to directly influence politics, the media, the economy, the judiciary, and the government;

- organized crime is often characterized by decentralization, flexibility, adaptability, use of modern technology, and high-level networking;
- organized crime is typically international rather than contained by state borders.

Some of the activities that organized crime is typically engaged in include arms trafficking, drug trafficking, smuggling of legal products to avoid taxes and duties, trafficking in persons, sexual slavery, computer crime, false accounting, illegal production and corruption. Many of these activities are made possible by the global economy and global financing. Human trafficking is now the third largest activity of organized crime in Europe after trafficking in drugs and arms. Human trafficking would exist without organized crime, but not at such a high level. One of the reasons that so many women and children are ensnared and sold into sexual slavery is because the networks used for human trafficking were already in place within several types of criminal organizations. There is thus a strong connection between drug trafficking and human trafficking.[2] Very often the same routes, same people, and same organizations are used for trafficking both drugs and women.[3] The fight against human trafficking is therefore a simultaneous attack on drug trafficking.

Criminal organizations vary in size and activities. Large criminal organizations are characterised by a hierarchical international structure with political and economic contacts at all levels in countries of origin, transit, and destination. These are the groups that organize trafficking in human beings and buy, sell and exploit victims of trafficking. Medium-sized organizations usually do not sell victims to other criminal groups. They buy victims and keep them under their control, placing them in their own clubs, brothels, saunas, strip-bars, and other locations. In general, smaller criminal organizations transfer victims across borders and sell them to bigger criminal organizations. These bigger criminal organizations then organize the direct exploitation of the victims, who are sometimes resold and transferred over yet another national border. The smaller and medium-sized organizations therefore support and increase the power of the larger organizations. These organizations all know and exploit the vulnerabilities of national legal systems. They know and use to their advantage the fact that certain countries have more corruptible police, a legal system that defines a fourteen year old child as an adult, more permissive visa laws, or more leniency towards offenders for sexual exploitation. Large organizations have an efficient network that operates outside of their country. For instance the Komisaruk/Mezheritsky ring, a notorious Ukrainian trafficking organization, which was broken up in May 2001 in the United States, worked with two seemingly legitimate travel agencies in Kiev: Sweet Tours and Art Life International. It was the job of the agencies to lure girls and young women to Mexico as an easy way of entering and working in the United States where they were promised jobs as nannies and models. They even tricked some of the young women into paying for their plane fare for what they thought would be their ticket to prosperity. Instead, upon arrival in Mexico City, they were met at the airport by complicit Mexican airport officials

who arranged to have them ushered through "immigration" and into the hands of waiting Ukrainian traffickers. The girls were then spirited away to Tijuana or Ensanada, a region in Mexico settled by Russian immigrants. There they were locked down for days or even weeks in gated villas to "prepare" them for their trip to the United States and delivery into the hands of their buyers and sexual bondage. Their "preparation" consisted of sexual brutality including rapes and beatings and psychological torture with the aim of making them obedient sex slaves.[4]

It is difficult to identify and trace criminal organizations, not only because they are transnational, but also because they also engage in legal activities. In order to better control and solve the problem of human trafficking, it is necessary to have better procedures to trace, identify, and fight organized crime in Europe and the rest of the world. Because of the "decentralized," diverse and international nature of organized crime, a single state cannot alone effectively grapple with the organized crime networks that operate within its boundaries, therefore the approach to fighting organized crime must be simultaneously regional and international. The "decentralized" nature of this criminal activity, along with the criminal use of sophisticated computer and communications technology, makes it easy for these activities to operate just

> *The Eastern European trafficking operations, from entrapment to transport, tend to be well-oiled monoethnic machines.*
>
> *Peter Landesman,*
> *"The Girls Next Door," New*
> *York Times Magazine, 1/25/04*

"under the radar" of law enforcement, and also to disperse in anticipation of a raid and reemerge elsewhere. The battle against organized crime must take place on several fronts: in local, regional, and international law enforcement, as well as through cooperative efforts between nations to achieve social and economic stability in the region. It is necessary to set up a system of international cooperation for the collection, processing, and sharing of information on criminal organizations within Europe, including systematic methods for identification and prosecution of organized crime. Targeting heads of organized crime, identifying and rooting out established "rings," and prosecuting criminals is extremely labor intensive and beyond the abilities of transitional countries on their own.

Notes:

1. A major conference on organized crime was held in Naples, Italy in 1994.
2. As noted by the Drug Enforcement Administration of the United States.
3. An example: boats that bring trafficked women from Albania to Italy return carrying cigarettes.
4. Peter Landesman, "The Girls Next Door," *New York Times Magazine*, January 25, 2004: 17.

Chapter 4

The Plight of Trafficking Victims

Striptease was the most dreadful. I was awfully ashamed to dance in front of those big groups of men who were looking at me like wolves. I always prayed for a short song for my turn, at least no longer than four minutes.

Dorina, a 16 year old trafficking victim from Moldova[1]

In Chapter 2, we discussed how women and children are lured into the hands of sex traffickers. They are usually ensnared in the midst of their efforts to make a better life for themselves or their families. They have seen people go abroad, find a job, and send money home. And they have seen people return and build bigger houses and buy fancy cars.[2] Others see this and are tempted by the possibility that they may be as lucky or that their children or relatives will be. It must be emphasized that many families have a completely naive approach towards migration. Truly believing that their family member will be successful and send money home, they enthusiastically encourage them to go abroad, and may thus inadvertently push women and girls into the hands of traffickers. A family is often ready to sell something valuable such as a car or apartment in order to pay for necessary documents or the cost of travel for a member of their family to go abroad. Unfortunately, in some cases a family member will even act as middleman and sell a relative to a trafficker.

We have seen what happens to those who are unlucky. Sometimes instead of sending money home, they return emotionally destroyed and sick. They end up as sex slaves and may find themselves miles from home in the hands of vicious traffickers. Even those who were willing to work as prostitutes never imagined they would be bought and sold, perhaps repeatedly, and end up in bondage to an "owner" to whom they are indentured or mere slaves. Some victims end up dead – either murdered by their exploiters when they became too problematic or no longer useful, or as the result of suicide.

Once they are sold, their "owners" tell the women and children that they must work for free until they have paid back their own purchase price and/or travel costs. They might also be sold from one "employer" to another. The trafficking victims are completely vulnerable as the traffickers have taken their documents, abused them, and threatened them and their families with harm if they try to escape. Their debt increases as the "owners" charge them for room, board, medical expenses, and fine them if they break "house rules."[3]

Women and children who are trafficked are subjected to appalling working conditions in which they are forced to provide sexual services to customers, and may be physically and mentally abused by the pimp or brothel owners.[4] Also, unprotected sex is always a threat; trafficked women in the sex industry have

> *It is very interesting how the mafia in Turkey deals with trafficked women. Sometimes, the women don't even realize they have fallen into the trafficking trap. Take the case of a young woman who arrived in Turkey to work as a shop clerk in a clothing store. Several weeks after she was on the job, her supervisor told her she must sell a certain number of items to work off her travel "debt." The more she worked, the larger her debt grew until it was impossible for her to ever pay it off. She was then forced by her "employer" into prostitution to pay this "debt."*
>
> *"Irregular Migration and Trafficking in Women: The Case of Turkey"*
> *IOM 2003*

little control over their working environments, which means that HIV/AIDS, as well as other sexually transmitted diseases, are immediate threats to their health and their lives.[5] Threat of disease is not the only thing the women have to worry about: there is also customer brutality, including cigarette burns, head injuries, and fractures.[6]

> *Traffickers transported her across a river by boat. Although she was promised a job harvesting tangerines in Greece, traffickers took her to Bosnia and Herzegovina. Traveling at night, two male escorts took her and several other women over a river by motorboat and then by car to a small house. There, traffickers ordered the women to undress. When she refused, one of the traffickers took her upstairs where he first beat and then raped her. She was then sold to the owners of a bar in Prijedor.*
>
> *Testimony of a 17 year old Romanian girl*
> *Human Rights Watch, "Report on Human Trafficking in Bosnia and Herzegovina 2002"*

WHERE TRAFFICKED VICTIMS WORK

There are many different establishments in which the sexual services of trafficked women and children may be made available to interested clients including brothels, hotels, apartments, night clubs, go-go bars, gay bars, salsa bars, restaurants, massage parlours, beauty salons, escort agencies, phone sex, and street prostitution. The clients and atmosphere in these establishments are different, as may be the conditions and treatment of the trafficked women and children who find themselves in such surroundings.

Closed Brothels

Women taken to closed brothels are usually young, illegal immigrants from Southeast Europe without documents. The closed brothels are in most cases a combination of a restaurant and hotel where the women's bedrooms are generally used for servicing clients. The working conditions in the closed brothels are the most oppressive. One trafficking victim described them in graphic terms.

> *The bedrooms, located in a small corridor*
> *behind the bar, reeked of perspiration and*
> *other bodily fluids. The bathrooms facilities were*
> *completely inadequate... Condoms littered the*
> *floor, and the bed sheets were dirty.*[7]

The owners are paid directly. As one trafficked woman described, "In 2000, I worked in Maskarada 3 months... I worked in Crazy Horse for a month for free, because Milka (the owner) bought me. She bought my clothes and provided me with food. I had 265 clients in 4 months...but Milka has never given me any money."[8]

Most closed brothels have strict rules with limited freedom of movement, minimal health care, and unprotected sex. Many women liberated by police raids described brothels as prisons. As one victim described her situation, "I was sold in Bosnia. The owner told me that he paid 2000 KM (1000 €) for each of seven girls. My movement was restricted completely. I could not go anywhere." [9]

The clients of this type of brothel tend to be less educated. In Southeast Europe the customers are generally lower middle-class. In Bosnia and Herzegovina, Serbia and Montenegro including Kosovo and Macedonia the visitors to this type of brothel are local people and foreign soldiers.

Open Brothels

The open brothel may be an apartment or a house, where several women work together. They have a kind of semi-independence that allows them to go shopping alone or even to a cinema. They live together in the apartment or house and give "hospitality" to clients; they may even prepare lunch or dinner for the customers - having some drinks and then sex. The pimp, who is also the owner or renter of the premises, manages all the details of the business.

Through their sex work, the women cover all the expenses of this "business." They may put aside a little bit of money and the rest goes to the pimp. Women in these establishments are primarily victims of trafficking or undocumented people who choose to work in such a place. Usually, the group is composed of women from Southeast Europe working under a local woman. This woman is the coordinator, employed by the pimp, and has no obligation to have sex with customers. The guests of this type of brothel tend to be upper middle-class men who have disposable income such as local politicians, small business owners, and well-paid clerks or high-ranking foreign soldiers in Bosnia and Herzegovina, Kosovo, and Macedonia.

There are several variations of the open brothel. For example, the women may be in an apartment or a house, and wait for a phone call to go to a certain address, which is usually a hotel. After several successful raids on bars in Bosnia and Herzegovina, the bar owners reorganized into this type of brothel. Another variation is set up as a link for a hotel, which, through an agent, provides women for sex. These women stay in a room in the hotel, and must be ready to receive clients at any time. The social level of the customer depends on the level of hotel.

Escort Agencies and Call-Girls

The most sophisticated form of prostitution is organized by escort agencies for which women serve only one client per day or night. The client may be a foreigner or a local person who is able to cover the expense. Usually, clients are from the business world, for some of them a relation with a call-girl is more then sex. As one client expressed it, "I like to be with her, she is smart and beautiful and, she knows a lot. After all of the stress I have in my life, it is very relaxing to be with her."[10] Another said, "I am alone, and I am a very busy man. Sometimes I need company, just to speak with somebody; sex is not obligatory but is welcome."[11]

Massage Parlors

Although massage parlors are legal, sex organized behind their front is illegal. In these establishments there is a lot of forced prostitution and slavery, where women from Southeast Europe work as slaves, as masseuses, and as prostitutes. Usually, they live at the workplace and have no rights to leave or communicate with anybody outside. Often the trafficked women and children are exposed to violence - particularly if they refuse to have sex without protection.

Men who frequent this type of salon are usually well aware of the situation of these women and often treat them brutally. The customers are from all backgrounds: from dockers to soldiers, from drug dealers to engineers.

Go-Go Bars

In Southeast Europe, these types of bars are generally very basic, with table or lap dancing full of sexual innuendo. The so-called "artists" are from the region and in many cases do not work voluntarily. In the go-go bars women usually dance nearly naked and are obliged to entice the customers into heavy drinking and sex. Sex takes place upstairs, in the bar, or at another location. One victim described life in the bar. "The girls were obliged to dance, drink a lot, and go into their rooms with anyone. We ate once a day and slept 5 to 6 hours per day. If we would not do what they wanted us to do, the security guards would beat us."[12]

The customers frequenting these bars tend to be local officials, local police, members of the new mafia clans, and those involved in business tied to irregular or criminal activities.

Escape

If a trafficking victim manages to escape, she faces the difficult challenge of finding help. She most likely does not speak the local language, has no money, no passport or visa, and no friends or family. She may be reluctant to go to the police since, for a trafficking victim, the police may represent a kind of mafia in uniform and, in some cases, victims' customers have been police officers or soldiers. An experienced IPTF human rights officer who had interviewed dozens of trafficked women told Human Rights Watch:

> *The trafficked women do not trust the local police. Very often the local police visit the clubs. They see local police every day, and some use their sexual services sometimes for free because they have connections to the owners. So the women don't trust the local police. They are threatened by the owners, who tell them that this policeman is his protection or 'roof.'[13]*

In general she will not know the rights to which she is entitled as a victim and not know how to contact agencies that can help support her with protection, medical, and legal assistance. If she contacts her embassy, she may or may not be offered the advice and assistance that could lead her to agencies which are set up to help trafficking victims. As discussed earlier, if she is picked up by the police in a raid or on the street, she may be put in jail, prosecuted as a prostitute, and denied the social services crucial to her extricating herself from her traffickers.

Some victims are fortunate enough to get help from international organizations, government agencies, and non governmental organizations (NGOs) that have established services to assist victims of trafficking. Services include medical care, shelter, legal aid, and psychological support. But many women and children are either unaware of these services or afraid to ask for help for fear of being sent home or discovered by their traffickers. If they do get help and protection, trafficked women can begin to rebuild their lives and also provide important information to assist in the identification and prosecution of traffickers. But many victims are simply deported and take back with them the psychological and physical trauma resulting from their experience additionally complicating an already difficult reentry.

Returning Home

Many trafficking victims say they want to return home but are sometimes afraid of coming into contact with their traffickers, as was this woman from Moldova.

> *I am afraid that he, my friend's brother, the person who sold me, will come and demand money from me. The police are corrupt there. They'll say that I was a prostitute and then the police won't help. He'll find out that I am home and demand more money...There is no phone in my village and I cannot call anyone...If he comes to my house and threatens me, I have no money to call Chisinau for help. (Chisinau is the capital of Moldova).[14]*

And upon returning home, some women do, indeed, end up being "retrafficked," - recaptured by their original traffickers who threaten and intimidate them and force them to once more go abroad as sex slaves.

Trafficking can have an effect not only on the woman or child who is trafficked, but also on the family and community. Many families search long and hard and often in vain to find their trafficked relatives. But because the victims have been given false passports with different names and ages, they can literally disappear.

> *"They have someone in Belgrade who makes false passports. The woman goes to the photographer and...they give her a passport, change her name, change her age...If her family searches for her they cannot find her...there is no such girl."*[15]

Some women are concerned about returning home to face their families and society. The reaction of the family can vary. Some try to keep the facts about the trafficking hidden because they are afraid of the reaction from the community. Others try to protect the victim because of what they have been through. Others completely ignore the situation and pretend like it never happened or is inconsequential. Also, the local community may blame the victim for having been trafficked and consider her a person of low morality. This can cause great strain on the victim, the family, and the community and alter relationships within the family and neighborhood.

Reintegration is a long and difficult process for trafficking victims. In order to regain their lives and dignity they require a great deal of help from their families and communities, including support from social services organized by those who understand the special needs of trafficking victims.

Notes:

1. *End Child Exploitation*, (UNICEF UK, 2003).
2. Interview with a waiter in a hotel in Kiev, Ukraine, 10 July 2003.
3. *Hopes Betrayed*, Human Rights Watch, Vol. 14, No. 9 (D), 2002: 16.
4. Ibid.
5. UNBIH press release, "Sex Industry Linked to Spread of HIV/AIDS in Southeastern Europe," U.N. Official, November 30, 2001. See: <http://www.unmibh.org/stories/11_2001/44.htm>.
6. *Hopes Betrayed* 18.
7. *Hopes Betrayed* 17.

8. IPTF official interview transcript, Prijedor #5, 22 November 2000. See: <http://www.humanrightswatch.org/reports/2002/bosnia/>.

9. ITPF internal report, Tuzla, 26 June 2000.

10. Interview with NN in 2003, NN is a successful businessman who runs a business in Eastern and Southeast Europe.

11. Interview with AA in 2003. AA is a frequent business traveler.

12. IPTF interview transcript, Prijedor #3, 22 November 2000. See: <http://www.humanrightswatch.org/reports/2002/bosnia/>.

13. See Amnesty International's report entitled: "So does it mean that we have the rights?" published in 2004. The report condemns the actions of international peacekeepers in Kosovo (UNMIK). See: <http://web.amnesty.org/library/Index/ENGEUR700102004?open&of=ENG-YUG>

14. *Hopes Betrayed* 19-20.

15. *Hopes Betrayed* 16-17.

Chapter 5

Why Southeast Europe Has Become a Center for Sex Trafficking

She was a Romanian citizen who wanted to go to Italy. She could not find a way to support herself at home and had a dream that she would find a better life there. She had money for neither passport nor visa, but she was told that close to the border she could find a man who could help her cross without these documents. So she went to Temishvar and met two young men who promised to organize her trip to Italy. But at the end of her relatively short journey, she found herself not in Italy but at the "Arizona" market in Bosnia and Herzegovina in a nightclub. She was stripped of her clothes and, naked, she was sold at auction. Before her owner registered her at the police station, he beat her up so that she would tell the police exactly what he wanted her to say - that she had voluntarily come to work in Bosnia and Herzegovina.[1]

In most countries of Southeast Europe, trafficking in women and children has reached epidemic proportions. It is not a fluke that women and children from this region in particular are being entrapped into forced prostitution and sexual slavery. Human trafficking has always been closely connected with economic factors and migration patterns, and, since the early 1990s, the countries of Southeast Europe have suffered from economic and social instability and decline, along with increasingly porous borders and mass migration in and around the region. Since the fall of the Berlin Wall in the early 1990s, tens of thousands of women from Eastern and Southeast Europe have taken their chances and entered Western Europe illegally, and many of those have ended up on the "market" as prostitutes and the victims of human trafficking.

"Arizona," a marketplace in Bosnia and Herzegovina, close to the border with Croatia and Serbia, was also used as a market for trafficked women and girls.

The transition from a state economy to a market economy has been a difficult one for the countries of Southeast Europe, particularly when combined with regional conflict and post-conflict political realities. The newly formed and transitional governments are often weak and in flux, and do not yet have tight controls, a well-run infrastructure, or consistent law enforcement in place. This has led to a flourishing black market economy, the corruption of government employees (including police and border guards), the spread of organized crime and the widespread smuggling of drugs, luxury products, arms, and people wishing to migrate. Unemployment has increased, salaries for the few jobs that do exist are low, there is a wider gap between rich and poor than before, and more and more people are living in poverty with substandard living conditions and minimal access to social services.

Women have been especially hard hit by these new economic and social norms. The level of unemployment among women is much higher than among men, more women live in poverty than men, and in worse conditions. Even when they can find work, it is often limited to "traditional women's work," where they earn significantly less money than men. This situation, known as the "feminization of poverty," can be found in many other regions in the world. Studies have shown that the feminization of poverty is a result of social, economic and political discrimination against women.[2] Women are denied access to economic resources more often than men - resources such as sources of income, ownership of property, inheritance, loans, and vocational skills training that will make them more qualified for employment.

This means that leaving the country to find work becomes an attractive option for many women, or may seem like the only option, especially if there are dependent family members to support. Economic factors are often combined with other factors that encourage the young women of Southeast Europe to migrate. There has been an increase in the level of violence

> *In Chisinau, the capital of the former Soviet republic of Moldova – the poorest country in Europe and the one experts say is the most heavily culled by traffickers for young women – I saw a billboard with a fresh-faced, smiling young woman beckoning girls to waitress positions in Paris. But of course there are no waitress positions and no "Paris."*
>
> *Peter Landesman, "The Girls Next Door" New York Times Magazine, 1/25/04*

against women in Southeast Europe, especially domestic violence. Women often have a difficult position in the family – on one hand, they may be responsible for the well-being of the family, especially economically, but on the other hand they are often excluded from decision-making processes within the family. Since the beginning of the transition, women have had less representation in government, and less and less influence on public and political life.

For these women, the West seems to offer better opportunities overall – not only the chance to find employment and make more money than is possible in Southeast Europe, but also to live a Western lifestyle, with a better quality of life, including less discrimination against women. This perception is enhanced by watching American and European movies and television programs, or reading articles about life in the West. But the images that these sources present tend to be glamorized, and show the benefits of migrating to the West to work, but almost never show the risks and costs of being an "irregular" immigrant – those without legal immigration status.

Women who have decided to leave the country for economic betterment become vulnerable to the snares of human traffickers. They are usually aware of the requirements for getting to the West - both legal and otherwise, and know that they will need a passport and help with buying or arranging visa documents, transportation, a job and a place to live. However, most of these migrating women are young, sometimes without much education, and without the experience of travel abroad. They don't understand the reality of life and work in the West, and don't have a basis of comparison for salaries and working conditions – they are unable to judge which offers are "too good to be true." In addition, they often move abroad alone, leaving them isolated and without the protection of family and friends. They have neither contacts nor a support system in the country to which they plan to immigrate.

Western European countries contribute to the problem of trafficking of Southeast European women and girls through their strict migration policies which make it difficult to get a residence or work permit. At the same time, there is a strong demand for immigrants and the cheap labor that they can provide. This demand for labor is the result of several factors including Western Europeans living longer, having lower birth rates, and their lack of interest in doing low prestige and low level labor. The restrictive migration policies, despite strong demand for migrant workers on the part of Western European countries, combined with the difficult economic situation in Southeast European countries and the desire of their citizens for a better life, creates a perfect situation for a flourishing black market in labor as it provides economic incentive for people to smuggle illegal immigrants into countries where they can find work.

This pattern of mass migration, along with systems of smuggling people, greatly facilitates human trafficking – many victims of human trafficking think that they are simply going to be smuggled into a Western European country for domestic or restaurant work, but end up being sold into slavery as sex workers. In some ways it merely comes down to luck – a woman may end up transported to Western Europe and set up with illegal employment, or may end up forced into prostitution and sexual slavery. The system of human smuggling, and the system of human trafficking that lurks just underneath, means that once a woman decides to migrate and place herself in the hands of smugglers there is no way for her to know which fate will be hers. The naivety, isolation, and powerlessness of women migrating out of Southeast Europe means that too many women who think that they are enroute to a better life in the West end up exploited and victimized by human traffickers.

Southeast Europe is now a prime location for the three stages of human trafficking. It is a region of origin in which women and children are ensnared by traffickers, shipped cross borders, and forced to work as prostitutes. It is a region of transit in which trafficking victims are smuggled through Southeast Europe en route to their final destination. While they are in transit they may also be sold and resold in one of the region's slave markets. Finally, Southeast Europe is a region of destination, where women and children are forced to provide sexual services for local men, international soldiers, and employees of international organizations.

To conclude, human trafficking is flourishing in Southeast Europe. Young women are driven by social and economic factors to migrate to the West, and the porous borders[3] and instability of Southeast European countries have contributed to mass, often irregular, migration within the region. The thriving black market, high level of organized crime and corruption mean that systems for all kinds of smuggling are in place, and human traffickers take advantage of these migration patterns and smuggling systems – the same routes and systems are used for trafficking women and trafficking drugs. This efficient system combined with a lack of interest in identifying and prosecuting human traffickers, deriving from the lack of adequate legislation, effective law enforcement systems and financial means, has led to a dramatic increase in the amount of human trafficking in Southeast Europe.

Notes:

1. Story told by an SFOR Officer in Bosnia and Herzegovina.
2. Barbara Limanowska, *Trafficking in Human Beings in Southeastern Europe* (Belgrade:UNICEF, UNOHCHR, OSCE/ODIHR, 2002) 5.
3. For example, in Bosnia and Herzegovina, only about 40 out of 432 border crossings were guarded when the State Border Service was established. According to reports made by the State Border Service, the situation concerning border security is improving but is still far from satisfactory.

Chapter 6

Why Isn't More Being Done
to Combat Human Trafficking?

The problem exists, but it should not be our priority. We could solve it completely, at least in the smaller communities, provided we are given such instructions.

Former police officer,
"Trafficking in Women and Children
for Sexual Exploitation" IOM, Zagreb 2002

The battle against human trafficking is a difficult one – the way it operates, and the social and economic systems that facilitate human trafficking are diverse and hard to pinpoint. What's worse, many people do not realize just how serious the issue of human trafficking is. They do not understand that a vulnerable part of their population is being siphoned off and forced to earn a profit for people who, in addition to abusing the human rights of their victims, only undermine the local economy rather than support it.

Most people, including government officials, simply do not recognise the seriousness of the phenomenon of human trafficking and sexual slavery. There are many factors that contribute to the inability or unwillingness to acknowledge the problem.

- Governments tend to avoid admitting that there is human trafficking and sexual slavery in their territory; this is true for countries that are sources, transit points, and destinations for trafficked women and girls.

- Victims of human trafficking come from developing or underdeveloped countries. The governments of these countries have "more important things" to take care of, other crises to attend to – fighting human trafficking is low on their list of priorities.

- The women and children who are trafficked often come from the lowest socio-economic levels of their country. Even if their families learn of their plight, they usually do not have the knowledge or resources to pressure governments, particularly on an international level.

- Prostitution is either a legal or tolerated phenomenon in some countries, and sexual slavery is sometimes neglected or equated with "paid sex," the latter being sometimes legal. Therefore, it seems that sexual slavery is becoming legitimate.

- Criminal codes do not recognize the severity of the crime of human trafficking, and often do not recognize human trafficking as a separate crime; human trafficking is treated as a less serious crime than drug trafficking or arms smuggling.

- Even if criminal codes were sufficient, prosecution and the execution of justice would still be uneven due to corruption and the influence of organized crime at various levels of government.

- Due to a lack of understanding of the nature of human trafficking, combined with the absence of appropriate laws and protocols, the victims of human trafficking are often treated as criminals, even though they themselves are the victims of crime.

- For many countries it is cheaper to treat trafficked people as criminals than to recognize them as victims of trafficking, which includes protection and assistance (safe accommodation, medical care and services, rehabilitation, etc.). This approach also undermines data collection on trafficking in women and girls.

- In many cases, diplomatic representatives of a victim's country of origin in a destination country don't want to communicate with the victim, in that way avoiding the responsibility to provide assistance such as translation, documents, money for travel, and accommodation.

- The lack of cooperation between diplomatic representatives and victims of trafficking leads to the deportation of victims by local authorities. Victims can be deported to other countries, regions, or state borders where that person usually once again becomes a victim of trafficking. Therefore, the fate of victims of trafficking more or less depends on the criminal code and activities of NGOs in destination countries.

- Lack of reliable and consistent data.

The problem with data is a pressing one. Even though the literature on the subject of trafficking in women is growing, reliable data on the number of trafficked people is very limited and the overall number of victims of trafficking in the EU is still unknown. The number of victims is surely higher than the official statistics of the EU Member States. For instance, in March 2001 the European Commission reported that approximately 120,000 women and children have been trafficked into Western Europe,[1] but the report did not give the sources for this number.

The EU has supported research in trafficking in Member States under the umbrella of the STOP Program (Sexual Trafficking of Persons). Their data comes from national law enforcement agencies, which are supplied with numbers by local and regional law enforcement offices. In reality, however, many of these local or regional offices pay little attention to human trafficking. Consequently, thus far, no scientifically reliable statistics about the number of victims of trafficking in EU Member States have been published.

The UN Center for International Crime Prevention (UNCICP) in Vienna is developing a database on people who are trafficked. After studying thousands of cases of human trafficking, the UNCICP reached the following conclusions: "Eighty to ninety percent of those trafficked become victims of sexual exploitation, the rest victims of forced labor…nearly half of the victims of trafficking were children, and 96 percent were females…there were some 700,000 to 1 million cases of human trafficking annually around the world."[2]

Yet some are skeptical of the validity of these numbers. Ann Jordan, the Director of the Initiative Against Trafficking in Persons of the International Human Rights Law Group, raised the issue, "The UN is constantly using the statistic of about 1 million people trafficked and it would be very useful to have some information on how this number is compiled. I know that a number of people have attempted to find its origin, without any success."[3]

The lack of data on trafficking on the European level is a reflection of the same factors mentioned above. It is also due to the fact that governments are able to avoid tackling the problem by pointing a finger at other countries and regions and saying that perhaps human trafficking can be found elsewhere - but not in their region. By doing this, they are ignoring the fact that trafficking in human beings is a global problem and represents a most serious violation of human rights.

Notes:

1. EC.2001:2.
2. *The Associated Press*, 14   May 2003.
3. *Stop-Traffic* (E-mail), 14 May 2003.

Chapter 7

Defining Human Trafficking

One of the problems with the international fight against trafficking in human beings is that there is no single agreed-upon definition of trafficking in human beings.

Human trafficking is an aspect of migration, and in the contemporary world it is primarily women and girls who are trafficked. At the beginning of the 20th Century, the League of Nations recognized this problem in a number of agreements designed to combat the sale of women and children. This phenomenon came to be known as the "white slave trade," because it was white women being sold into prostitution.

In 1949, the UN General Assembly approved a new convention to replace the earlier international conventions of 1904,[1] 1910,[2] 1921,[3] and 1933.[4] The new convention was the Convention for the Suppression of Traffic in Persons and of the Exploitation of Prostitution of Others. However, this treaty was not widely ratified and has been criticized for its lack of a clear definition of trafficking, lack of enforcement mechanisms, and for addressing trafficking as solely the cross-border movement of people into prostitution. Due to the lack of clarity in the convention, "trafficking" has often been lumped together with prostitution as a form of exploitation. Additionally, the convention did not include trafficking for other purposes, and did not cover all contemporary forms of trafficking. However, after 1947 several international treaties were adopted which did address the more complex context of trafficking.

As the scale of human trafficking increased in the 1990s, more attention was paid to the phenomenon. The lack of a clear definition of trafficking in the 1949 Convention led various organizations to adopt their own definitions.

For instance, the November 1996 European Commission Communication on Trafficking in Women for the Purpose of Sexual Exploitation defined trafficking for sexual exploitation in this way:

> *Trafficking for the purpose of sexual exploitation covers women who have suffered intimidation and/or violence through trafficking. Initial consent may not be relevant, as some enter the trafficking chain knowing they will work as prostitutes, but who are then deprived of their basic human rights, in conditions which are akin to slavery.*

The definition points out that the women who enter the EU through both regular or irregular channels can be considered to have been trafficked.

A 1998 Communication from the European Commission[5] noted that the definition should be changed:

by including also women who are trafficked abroad and forced to perform other forms of commercialized sex than prostitution, as well as women who are forced into marriage for the purpose of sexual commercial exploitation.

The International Organization for Migration (IOM) adopted its definition in May 1999, which states that trafficking exists when:

migrants illicitly engaged (recruited, kidnapped, sold, etc.) and/or moved, either within national or across international borders;[and] intermediaries (traffickers) during any part of this process obtain economic or other profit by means of deception, coercion, and/or other forms of exploitation under conditions that violate the fundamental rights of migrants.

The IOM definition greatly contributed to a movement away from the 1949 Convention and the adoption of a new international standard, the Trafficking Protocol. As of December 2000, The United Nations Convention Against Transnational Organized Crime, accompanied by protocols on trafficking and smuggling (The Protocols) [6] had been signed by 124 states. The smuggling protocol has been signed by 78 states, and the trafficking protocol has been signed by 81 states.

In the period between 1990 and 2000 there was much debate on the question: "who is a victim of trafficking, and who is not a victim of trafficking?" This is because there is no clear distinction between "voluntary" prostitution and forced prostitution, or between smuggling and trafficking. Instead, they can be viewed as a continuum:

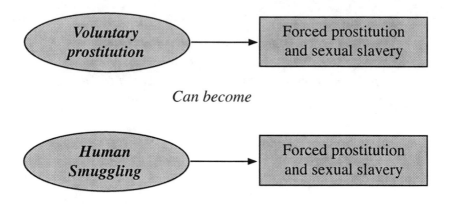

In the Protocols of 2000, the UN defined two distinct terms "trafficking" and "smuggling" as follows:

> *'Trafficking in persons' shall mean the recruitment, transportation, transfer, harbouring or receipt of persons, by means of the threat or use of force or other forms of coercion, of abduction, of fraud, of deception, of the abuse of power or of a position of vulnerability or of the giving or receiving of payments or benefits to achieve the consent of a person having control over another person, for the purpose of exploitation. Exploitation shall include, at a minimum, the exploitation of the prostitution of others or other forms of sexual exploitation, forced labor or services, slavery or practices similar to slavery, servitude or the removal of organs.*

> *'Smuggling of migrants' shall mean the procurement, in order to obtain, directly or indirectly, a financial or other material benefit, of the illegal entry of a person into a State Party of which the person is not a national or a permanent resident.*

"Smuggling" is seen here as the irregular transportation of a person or group of persons across a state border bringing benefit/profit to the smuggler. This definition mentions only the transport of a person across the border for profit. This suggests that exploitation during transportation does not exist, which is not always the case. The person smuggled is very often in a situation in which there is a high risk of injury or even death. Therefore, smuggling can be seen as human rights abuse, but it is important to note that smugglers do not have the abuse of the person being transported as their intent.

By definition, "trafficking" implies that the trafficked person is an object of exploitation. From the beginning of the operation, the aim is the exploitation of a person in order to make a profit. Along with trafficking comes abduction, coercion, fraud, deception etc. But trafficking may include elements of smuggling. According to the UN definition, trafficking can, though this is not always the case, include elements of international migration. For example, trafficking may involve crossing a state border, but can also take place within a country, for example movement from a rural to a more urban area. Here is a summary of the differences between smuggling and trafficking:

SMUGGLERS	TRAFFICKERS
• provide service for a (high) price	• buy and sell people
• organize transfer of people emigrating or seeking asylum – there is no further contact after the migrant is delivered to the agreed-upon destination	• sometimes provide a service to the people being smuggled, but exploit them for labor, including forced prostitution • victims are often dehumanized into consumer goods that are delivered and sold for a profit
• services include: hiding people in vehicles, bribing officers, serving as guides	• intimidate and abuse the people they are smuggling through rape, beatings and other forms of violence

Some experts have expressed reservations about the definitions found in the UN Protocols.[6]   They have noted that in some cases it is quite difficult to make a distinction between smuggling and trafficking. There are ways in which a smuggled person can be exposed to violation and exploitation during transportation to the destination or after arriving at the destination. An example would be irregular migrants who die during smuggling or upon arrival.[7]

In addition, it is sometimes very difficult to clearly divide migrant women into two distinct groups – those who are trafficked and those who are smuggled. Several studies have shown that many women who decided to go abroad were already aware of the risks involved. On the other hand, in many current public debates, all women who work as prostitutes abroad are considered to be victims of trafficking. Both perceptions are incomplete. In fact, it is often difficult to differentiate between a woman who is a victim of trafficking and a woman who is not.

In some cases, a woman decides to go abroad knowing that she will work in the sex industry. But then the conditions in which she has to work change and become unacceptable to her: conditions such as a payment of debt, number of clients, limits on freedom, sex without protection, etc. When she is forced to work under these conditions she can be considered a victim of trafficking. But another woman faced with the same changes might find that these new conditions are acceptable to her. We are then faced with the question: "Is she or is she not a victim of trafficking because she can accept the conditions in which she is working?"

Another issue is how to consider a woman who pays a smuggler to help her cross a border to work as prostitute. She does not depend on anybody; she works alone and after a while returns home with some money. What does a smuggler or trafficker represent for this woman involved in prostitution? Research has shown that even though they are exploiters, women may also see them as helpful.

Finally, it is necessary to think about just how "voluntary" voluntary prostitution really is. Research has shown that many women enter the sex industry because of "dire economic need" they exist in a social context where employment options are extremely limited.[8] Entering into prostitution may seem the least bad of the few options for a woman who simply has no other way to put a roof over her head, feed her family, or escape from domestic abuse.

Although these questions show just how complicated migrant prostitution is, their discussion should not in any way discourage the fight against human trafficking. At the beginning of this chapter we outlined the problem of defining trafficking in human beings, but there are some elements common to most definitions:

- Human trafficking is a fundamental violation of human rights.
- Human trafficking leads to exploitation and forced labor – this labor is often prostitution in slavery-like conditions.
- Human trafficking involves the recruitment of women and girls for the purpose of prostitution or involvement in other forms of the sex-industry, and they are often transported across national borders, sometimes legally.
- Human trafficking often begins with deception.
- Human trafficking preys upon the weak: traffickers capitalize on the hopeless situation of women and girls in their home countries.
- Human trafficking produces victims. Even women who have decided to work in the sex industry abroad because they are in a desperate economic situation do not expect the miserable, violent, dangerous enslavement that they can end up in once they put their fate into the hands of traffickers.

To sum up, the key elements of human trafficking are:

- the recruitment, transportation, harbouring, transfer, and receipt of people;
- threats, coercion, force, fraud, and deception;
- the placement of people in slavery, slavery-like conditions, and forced labor services including: forced prostitution and other sexual services, domestic servitude, bonded sweatshop labor, other debt bondage.

Notes:

1. International Agreement of 18 May 1904 for the Suppression of the White Slave Traffic.
2. International Convention of 4 May 1910 for the Suppression of the White Slave Traffic.
3. International Convention of 30 September 1921 for the Suppression of the Traffic in Women and Children.
4. International Convention of 11 October 1933 for the Suppression of Traffic in Women.
5. Communication from the Commission to the Council and the European Parliament, For Further Actions in the Fight Against Trafficking in Women; COM (1998) 22, Brussels, 1998.
6. UN Protocol to Prevent, Suppress and Punish Trafficking in Persons, Especially Women and Children, supplementing the United Nations Convention against Transnational Organized Crime and the Protocol against the Smuggling of Migrants by Land, Sea and Air, supplementing the United Nations Convention against Transnational Organized Crime.
7. Susanne Thorbek, "Prostitution in a Global Context: Changing Patterns" *Transnational Prostitution*, ed. Susanne Thorbeck and Bandana Pattanaik (London: Zed Books Ltd, 2002) 5.
8. Ibid.

Chapter 8

How Do We Solve the Problem of Human Trafficking and Sexual Slavery?

In this book you have learned about the system of human trafficking in Southeast Europe and its negative effect not only on the individual victims of trafficking, but also on the region as a whole as it undermines the economic and social systems. The system of human trafficking is perpetuated and facilitated by other negative systems and situations: the economic and political difficulties of most of the countries of Southeast Europe, economic inequality with neighbouring countries, the black market and the black market of labor, the unfavorable position of women and girls, and irregular mass migration to the countries of Western Europe.

Unfortunately, it is still difficult to completely comprehend the size and severity of the problem of human trafficking because there simply is not enough data. If we are really going to understand and thus be able to combat trafficking effectively, information gathering and analysis needs to become systematic, methodical, and structured in the same way in each country – and information needs to be shared among all the countries affected by human trafficking.[1]

But, in the meantime, are there steps that can be taken to help solve the problem of human trafficking in Southeast Europe? Because the problem has so many angles, takes place in so many countries, and so many different kinds of people are involved, one may think, "This problem is just too complex – how can we possibly fix it?" But there is concrete action that can be taken at every level of government, by the police, and even by ordinary citizens to help attack the system of trafficking and assist the women and children who are victims of this terrible form of exploitation. The focus must be in three areas:

- Prevention
- Protection
- Prosecution

There are different ways to prevent women and girls from becoming victims of human trafficking; ways that victims can be protected and assisted; and ways to improve the prosecution of traffickers so that in the future human trafficking will no longer be a low-risk/high-profit criminal enterprise.

PREVENTION

Informational campaigns and awareness raising[2]

Potential victims of trafficking, including school children, and particularly women and children applying for passports and visas, need to be educated about the dangers of trafficking and the ways that they can be ensnared. Informational campaigns also need to be directed at government officials such as embassy workers and police officers in destination countries so that they understand the problem of human trafficking, how to correctly identify victims of trafficking, and how to direct victims to the proper avenues of assistance. Finally, such information should be directed at potential customers to make them aware that they may be employing the services of trafficked women and girls who are held as slaves. Any campaign should include information about:

- The real opportunities for migration and employment in Western Europe. For example, what are the actual jobs and salaries available for women migrating out of Southeast Europe? What kinds of jobs and salaries are too good to be true, and thus simply being used as bait by traffickers rather than real jobs?

- What can happen in the process of migration, and how smuggling of migrants can easily turn into human trafficking for forced labor and forced prostitution.

- Health dangers associated with the sex industry, especially sexually transmitted diseases and HIV/AIDS.

Improvement in the social and economic situation
for women in Southeast Europe

Studies have shown that the majority of women who choose to migrate are escaping untenable economic situations, violence at home, or both. Illegal migration places these women at risk for entrapment by traffickers; a risk that could be avoided if they were able to live safely at home with decent jobs that provide a living wage. Here are some steps that could be taken to improve the position of women in the region:

- Fight domestic violence in Southeast Europe. The level of domestic violence in the countries of Southeast Europe has greatly increased in the last decade, and this is one of the major factors that cause women to choose risky emigration over staying at home in an abusive situation. Protection from domestic violence is an issue of human rights.[3] The countries of Southeast Europe need to develop a comprehensive plan to combat violence against women in the home and society.

• Promote gender equality, particularly in the labor force. Women in Southeast Europe disproportionately suffer from the difficult economic situation – their unemployment rates are higher, their salaries, when they do work, are lower, and they are often segregated into lower-paid, lower-prestige, and less-secure work "traditionally reserved for women." In addition, during the transition the number of women in governmental positions in Southeast Europe dropped dramatically. Therefore, strategies for economic improvement in Southeast Europe must take gender into account in order to address this inequity.

• Develop microcredit programs. Microcredit – small loans given to "micro entrepreneurs," people who run very small businesses – has been proven to be a successful way to provide women with attractive local options for better work so they don't have to migrate. Micro-credit organizations (which can be banks or religious organizations) offer small loans either directly to an individual or to a "community bank," which has an inter-dependent system in place to guarantee that loans will be paid back – group responsibility and group pressure means that the repayment rate can be over 99%. Some micro-credit organizations specifically target women: for example, "Mikra," a microcredit organization in Bosnia and Herzegovina that is run by the religious charity Catholic Relief, makes loans only to female entrepreneurs.[4] Microcredit loans can be used for rural businesses, for example, to buy farm animals, or for urban businesses to buy goods that can be sold in the local market. Most importantly, microcredit loans are successful – they allow women whose businesses are too small to qualify for a traditional bank loan to create job opportunities that allow them to support themselves and their families.

Change in immigration laws and policies in destination countries

It has been shown that restrictive immigration laws and policies in destination countries contribute to illegal migration, and thus also contribute to trafficking in women and girls. When women and children in Southeast Europe decide that they need to migrate in order to have a better life, but legal migration is not an option because of restrictive policies, they turn to smugglers, who claim that they will facilitate illegal migration, but may turn out to be traffickers who then force the women into sexual slavery. If destination countries were to allow more opportunities for women to immigrate legally, and worked in conjunction with countries of origin, this would most likely lessen incidences of human trafficking.

PROTECTION AND ASSISTANCE

Victim protection and assistance are directly related to the prosecution of traffickers: in order to build cases against traffickers and provide testimony in person, victims need to be assisted, stabilized, and protected. There are three major components to this process:

- victim identification
- victim assistance
- victim protection.

VICTIM IDENTIFICATION

Protocols and guidelines need to be developed to enable police and other officials to identify and assist trafficked victims effectively. Trafficked women and girls are only able to access assistance and protection after they have been identified as victims. There are currently six ways that victims are identified:

1. The victim is picked up in a police raid on a bar, brothel, night-club, hotel, sauna, or studio for massage, etc.
2. The victim is picked up during regular police document controls for example: on the street, at traffic checkpoints, or during bar inspections for working conditions.[5]
3. The victim escapes and turns to the police or her national embassy for help.
4. A client of the brothel/bar/night-club informs the police.
5. Parents, friends, or family ask for help from an NGO, the police, government and its diplomatic or consular representatives, or politicians.
6. The contract with the "owner" is terminated, and the victim is allowed to depart, after which she goes to the police or her embassy.

However, currently only a few countries have guidelines or protocols for local police to identify trafficking victims or put them in contact with the appropriate victim assistance services. It is estimated that 65% of trafficked women and children are not identified as victims, and are not referred for victim assistance. In addition, only 7% of trafficked women and children end up receiving long-term assistance with reintegration.[6]

VICTIM ASSISTANCE

Systems need to be developed that ensure that all women who are victims of trafficking receive both short-term and long-term assistance. IOM provides assistance for many victims of trafficking, but only for those people who are willing to return to their country of origin. If a woman is not willing to return or can't decide at the moment, she isn't recognized as a victim of trafficking, and doesn't qualify for assistance.[7] This needs to be changed. Women who do decide to return to their countries of origin need to be provided with good long-term assistance in reintegration – without this assistance, many returned victims face both the same lack of opportunities as before and new social problems such as ostracism. Between 30 and 50% of women and girls who are victims of trafficking and are returned home without good reintegration services end up either being trafficked again or working in the sex industry abroad.[8] Reintegration programs should include medical and psychological assistance, protection, vocational training, assistance in finding a job, and possibilities for microcredit for potential entrepreneurs. These reintegration programs need to be supported by the National Plan of Action for each country of origin and backed up by government cooperation with NGOs.

Destination countries should provide trafficked persons with legal residence status – these countries are reluctant to provide such status, even though this is an issue of human rights since many trafficked women face danger from traffickers upon returning home. Destination countries could use "humanitarian residence permits," as some countries have done, on either a temporary or permanent basis, and should also consider granting asylum in some cases.[9]

VICTIM PROTECTION

Programs for victim protection and witness protection need to be developed in both destination and origin countries. In destination countries, victims need a safe place to live, protection from traffickers, and assistance with stabilization so they can serve as witnesses for the prosecution of traffickers. In countries of origin, victims and their families need to be protected from retribution from traffickers.

The following example illustrates how opportunities to assist victims and acquire vital information about traffickers can slip away when there is no operational system in place to deal with a situation where human trafficking is suspected.

On July 25, 2005, "Daily Avaz," a newspaper in Bosnia and Herzegovina, reported that a policeman from Ilijas rescued a young woman from drowning in the River Bosna. She and a man had jumped into the river after their car crashed and the police arrived on the scene to assist them. The man was not found, but the young woman was taken to a clinic for treatment. She had no documents and initially didn't want to give any information about herself. Eventually she told the police that she was 26, that she had first come to BiH in 1998, was deported in 2002, and was now returning. She also explained that she had lived in the small town of Kiseljak near Sarajevo. She said she knew nothing about the man with whom she was traveling – that she had merely hitched a ride with him.

Two days later, another daily, "Nezavisne novine" (Independent news), reported the same story, but that the police, who suspected that the

young woman was a prostitute, had at this point
released her without cause. The police also told
the newspaper that she was Russian.[10]

There are many unanswered questions regarding the incident, especially given the fact that the police suspected the young woman was a prostitute. What happened to her documents, and how did she manage to enter Bosnia and Herzegovina without them? Why had she been deported in 2002? Why did she jump in the river? What happened to the man who was traveling with her? Was he perhaps a trafficker or pimp who was transporting her back into Bosnia and Herzegovina? Why didn't the police contact IOM or La Strada or other NGOs for assistance? Had the police asked these questions and coordinated with one of the NGOs to provide assistance, they might have helped the woman and also learned valuable information about trafficking into Bosnia and Herzegovina.

PROSECUTION

Prosecution of human traffickers is a means of prevention: prosecuting traffickers and imposing heavy criminal sentences should not only remove them from the system of trafficking, but also serve as a deterrent for other traffickers. Unfortunately, there are many obstacles that make the prosecution of human traffickers exceedingly difficult.

One major problem is with the legal systems within which traffickers would be prosecuted. Many countries do not have a legal code in which human trafficking is a distinct criminal offence. In these countries, traffickers are prosecuted under existing laws (such as laws against smuggling or prostitution-related crime), or they are not prosecuted at all. Sometimes prosecution is limited to traffickers who force victims into prostitution and excludes traffickers who exploit their victims with forced domestic and factory labor, forced servitude, or other sexual services such as pornography and striptease. Finally, even if human traffickers are convicted, they face only minor penalties, which are not at all proportionate to the severity of the crime – sentences are often only months, or a year or two – sentences for drug traffickers are ten times longer.

Another major problem with prosecution of traffickers lies in the enforcement of legal codes. Prosecution relies upon judges who may not understand the nuances of the complex laws used to fight trafficking, and who may not also understand just what human trafficking is. Corruption on the part of judges and police may mean that traffickers are not prosecuted or given only a slap on the wrist. The lack of witness protection programs means that women and children are often afraid to testify due to fear of revenge. Sometimes they leave behind written testimony, but this testimony lacks force in a courtroom setting, especially if a trafficker has witnesses present who have been recruited to vouch for his or her character.

There are several ways to overcome these problems with legal codes and their enforcement:

- The international community needs to develop and confirm a standard definition of trafficking, and to harmonize legislation taking into account the trans-border nature of trafficking movements.

- The legal codes of every country in Southeast Europe should conform with regard to trafficking. Each of these states needs to sign and ratify important international documents on trafficking, including:

  - The UN Convention against Trans-national Organized Crime and its supplementing Protocol to Prevent, Suppress and Punish Trafficking in Persons, especially Women and Children; also the Protocol against the Smuggling of Migrants by Land, Sea and Air;

- The UN Convention on the Elimination of All Forms of Discrimination Against Women and its Optional Protocol, which allows individual complaints and commissions of inquiry;

- The UN Convention on the Rights of the Child as well as the Optional Protocol on the Sale of Children, Child Prostitution and Child Pornography;

- The UN Convention on the Rights of Migrant Workers and their Families;

- The European Convention on Extradition and UN Crime Convention.

- The CoE Convention on Action Against Trafficking in Human Beings.

• The countries of Southeast Europe need to fight corruption of the police and the judiciary , this will have positive effects beyond the fight against trafficking,

• The police and the judiciary need to be trained about anti-trafficking laws and how they can be applied and enforced.

• Anti-trafficking measures should include the confiscation of assets and shutting down of legal enterprises run by traffickers.

• Ministries of Foreign Affairs need to be more active in trafficking issues by creating diplomatic networks among diplomats in embassies and consulates that are in destination countries for their trafficked citizens.

Finally, countries should consider prosecution of customers who employ the services of trafficked women and children. If there were no market, there would be no sexual slavery, thus those who participate in the market of sexual slavery must bear responsibility.

These measures, if enforced, would go a long way to stemming the tide of illegal trade in women and children from Southeast Europe.

Notes:

1.The United States is developing a program for information gathering and analysis that can be used as a role model; this program is run by the International Institute of Implementation of Law on Human Rights, which is working with the Inter-American Committee for Women and the Inter-American Institute of Children.

2. Many international organizations and protocols recommend informational anti-trafficking campaigns, along with informational campaigns that promote respect and equality for women, including the Convention on the Elimination of All Forms of Discrimination Against Women (CEDAW); The United Nations Trafficking Protocol; The Hague Ministerial Declaration of the European Union; the council of Europe Committee of Ministers.

3. Many conferences and international organizations promote the development of programs that fight domestic violence: e.g., The United Nations, The Convention on the Elimination of All Forms of Discrimination Against Women, and the Council of Europe's European Convention on Human Rights. In 1997, the Council of Europe set out a comprehensive plan to combat violence against women.

4. For more information on "Mikra," see <http://www.catholicrelief.org/ where_we_work/eastern_europe_&_the_caucasus/bosnia_and_herzegovina/ mikra.cfm>. More information on microcredit can be found at <www. katalysis.com> and at <www.grameen-info.org/mcredit/unreport.html>.

5. The first two ways are the most common methods of victim identification.

6. Barbara Limanowska, *Trafficking in Human Beings in Southeast Europe,* (Belgrade: UNICEF, UNOHCHR, OSCE/ODIHR, 2002) 141-143.

7. The authors spoke with representatives of IOM who explained that there are no qualifications for assistance and they emphasized that IOM gives help to all women who are in trouble.

8. Limanowska, 141-143.

9. This humanitarian temporary residence status has been recommended by the Council of Europe and is required by a 1997 Council Joint Action of the European Union, as well as resolutions by the European Parliament in 1989, 1993, 1996, and 2000. Italy and the Netherlands already provide temporary residence permits for victims of human trafficking.

10. *Dnevni Avaz*, 25 July 2005 and *Nezavisne novine* (Independent news), 27 July 2005.

Chapter 9

Action by the International Community to Combat Trafficking in Human Beings

The development of communications and the economic imbalance in the world have made trafficking more international than ever. First there was the white slave traffic, then trafficking from South to North, and now there is trafficking in human beings from less developed regions to more prosperous ones, whatever their geographical location (but in particular to Western Europe). The international community has recognized this phenomenon and has taken actions to combat it. There are a number of international agencies and organizations working on the issue of human trafficking; these agencies and organizations are described in this chapter.

UNITED NATIONS (UN)

The Member States of the United Nations have stressed that trafficking in human beings is a flagrant violation of victims' fundamental rights. They have noted that trafficking has become a major activity of international organized crime and called for the elimination of this phenomenon and assistance to the victims of this form of violence, who are mainly women and girls.

The United Nations has held numerous anti-trafficking conventions and created reports, resolutions and programs of action. In 1949, the UN General Assembly approved a new Convention for the Suppression of Traffic in Persons and of the Exploitation of Prostitution of Others. The new Convention replaced the earlier international conventions (see Chapter 5). Then in 1979, the UN General Assembly approved the Convention on the Elimination of all Forms of Discrimination against Women,[1] and in 1989 the Convention on the Rights of the Child.[2] Both of these conventions call on the member states to fight against sexual exploitation – in the first convention, against the exploitation of women; in the second convention, against the exploitation of children.

Other actions taken against trafficking include the very important Vienna Program of action, adopted by the World Conference on Human Rights in June 1993, and the Declaration on the Elimination of Violence Against Women adopted by the General Assembly in December of the same year. The 1994 Cairo Program of Actions and the 1995 Beijing Platform for Action, which established an Additional Protocol to the Convention on the Rights of the Child (adopted in 2000), also deserve attention.

However, these treaties have not been sufficient to combat the growing phenomenon of trafficking in human beings. Therefore, in December 2000 the UN opened for signature in Palermo the Convention against Transnational Organized Crime and its two Protocols (see Chapter 5). Some other United Nations activities related to trafficking include:

1. Since 1997, The UN High Commissioner for Human
    Rights (UNHCHR) has taken an active interest in
    the problem of trafficking in human beings, focusing
    in particular on trafficking in women and children.[3]
    UNHCHR is currently in the process of developing
    guidelines for the integration of human rights into
    national, regional and international anti-trafficking
    initiatives.

2. In 1999, a joint UNHCHR/Council of Europe Trafficking
    Prevention Program for Eastern and Central Europe
    was launched.

3. In Athens in 2000, UNHCHR and the Council of Europe
    worked together on the organization of a seminar aimed
    at developing a sub-regional plan of action against
    trafficking in human beings in Southeast Europe.

4. In Budapest in 2001, The United Nations Children Fund
    (UNICEF) in cooperation with the Council of Europe
    organized the Budapest Preparatory Conference for
    Europe on the Protection of Children Against Sexual
    Exploitation.

5. In December 2001, UNICEF co-sponsored the Second
    Congress Against Commercial Sexual Exploitation of
    Children in Yokohama, Japan.

INTERNATIONAL LABOR ORGANIZATION (ILO)

The ILO is very active on the issue of trafficking in human
beings with regard to forced labor, abuse of migrant workers,
discrimination at work, and child labor. The ILO addresses
trafficking in human beings through its Forced Labor Convention[4]
and the Worst Forms of Child Labor Convention.[5] In its 2001

report "Stopping Forced Labor," the ILO identified current problems of forced labor and trafficking throughout Europe. The ILO is currently developing a program to combat trafficking in children and young people for labor and sexual exploitation in the Balkans and Ukraine.

INTERNATIONAL ORGANIZATION FOR MIGRATION (IOM)

IOM is an organization focussing on the areas of trafficking prevention and assistance for the victims of trafficking. In May 2001, IOM signed a Memorandum of Understanding with the SECI Center in the field of assistance to repatriated trafficked women in the Balkan region. The aim of IOM is to help trafficked persons return voluntarily to their countries of origin. IOM has put together several reports concerning migration and trafficking in human beings. These reports emphasize:

- the illegal nature of this new form of slavery
- the lack of adequate legislation in many countries of the world concerning trafficking
- problems with testimony of victims of trafficking.

INTERPOL

Interpol is responsible for promoting cooperation and mutual assistance between criminal police authorities. In that regard, Interpol should play a major role in combating trafficking. In accordance with the terms of reference, Interpol has adopted a multidisciplinary approach calling for the coordination of the activities of all relevant authorities.

UNITED NATIONS ORGANIZATION FOR EDUCATION, SCIENCE AND CULTURE (UNESCO)

UNESCO is presently developing a new tool for people working on human trafficking issues, The UNESCO Trafficking Statistics Project. This is a first step towards clarifying what we know, what we think we know, and what we do not know about trafficking. UNESCO is tracing the origin of numbers of citations by various sources, attempting to ascertain the methodology by which these numbers were calculated, and evaluating their validity.

ORGANIZATION FOR SECURITY AND COOPERATION IN EUROPE (OSCE)

The OSCE plays a very important role in anti-trafficking work. Specific actions taken by OSCE include:

1. providing training and capacity building for NGOs
2. raising public awareness
3. ensuring victim support
4. developing regional cooperation.

With its 55 Member States, OSCE is the biggest organization for regional security in the world. Since the beginning of the 1990s, OSCE has been engaged in a number of activities to fight against trafficking in human beings in the fields of law enforcement, public awareness, and research, training and support for NGOs. In Moscow in 1991 the CSCE[6] Member States recognized the need to eliminate every form of violence against women, including trafficking.[7] In 1999, the Charter for European Security, adopted in Istanbul, redefined trafficking not only as trafficking in women but also as general trafficking in any human being.[8]

The OSCE Member States also recognized the need for implementation of relevant legislation to prosecute trafficking and to protect victims. In the Vienna Ministerial Council in 2000, the OSCE Member States made the decision that the countries of origin, transit and destination for trafficking in human beings should fight together against trafficking. This decision defines trafficking in human beings as: "an abhorrent human rights abuse and a serious crime." [9] At the Bucharest Ministerial Council on December 4, 2001, the OSCE proposed to its Member States that they should support investigations, law enforcement and crime prevention relating to trafficking.[10]

The OSCE Office for Democratic Institutions and Human Rights (OSCE/ODIHR) anti-trafficking activities target the prevention of trafficking and the protection of human rights. In this context ODIHR designed the "Reference Guide for Anti-Trafficking Legislative Review." In 2001, the OSCE adopted Anti-Trafficking Guidelines and expanded its Code of Conduct.[11]

THE COUNCIL OF EUROPE (CoE)

The Council of Europe (CoE) focuses on three areas of trafficking:

1. Legal reform
2. Law enforcement
3. Victim assistance.

The CoE is a European institution with 46 members - all European states are members except for Belarus. The CoE is responsible for issues of human rights and rule of law in Europe. Many CoE countries are countries of origin, transit and destination for human trafficking. In the early 1990s, the CoE and its Steering Committee for Equality Between Women and Men (CDEG) started paying considerable attention to trafficking in human beings.

The CDEG has organized different types of anti-trafficking activities, such as a seminar on trafficking in women and forced prostitution as violations of human rights and human dignity (Strasbourg 1991). As a result of this work, a Plan of Action against trafficking in women and forced prostitution (EG (96) 2) was prepared. This Plan of Action created the first true platform for government action. The CDEG has also organized an international seminar and workshops, including several seminars in a number of countries of origin. Under the authority of the CDEG, a group on action against trafficking in human beings for the purpose of sexual exploitation (EG-S-TS) was established.

In 1991, the Committee of Ministers of the CoE adopted Recommendation No R (91) 11 concerning sexual exploitation, pornography and prostitution of, and trafficking in, children and young adults. In this document, the CoE invited Member States to adopt specific measures related to trafficking, such as the supervision of the activities of various agencies and police-end protection of victims. The trafficking recommendation also proposed the exchange of information between countries throughout Europe and the creation of a European register of missing children.

The Committee of Ministers of the CoE adopted several additional recommendations relating to trafficking in the Declaration adopted at the Second Summit of the CoE (October 1997), in which the heads of state and governments of the member states of the CoE decided "to seek common responses to the challenges posed by the growth ..in organized crime..throughout Europe" and affirmed their determination "to combat violence against women and all forms of sexual exploitation of women." These include Recommendation No. R (96) 8, Recommendation No. R (97) 13, and Recommendation No. R (91) 11. Also the Committee of Ministers adopted Recommendation No. R (2000) 11 on action against trafficking in human beings for the purpose of sexual exploitation and Recommendation No. R (2001) 16 on the protection of children against sexual exploitation.

The Parliamentary Assembly of the Council of Europe has also adopted some recommendations and resolutions: Rec. 1065 (1987) on the trafficking of children and other forms of child exploitation; Rec. 1211 (1993) on clandestine migration relating to traffickers and employers of clandestine migrants;

Rec. 1325 (1997) on trafficking in women and forced prostitution in Council of Europe Member States; Rec. 1545 (2002) on a campaign against trafficking in women; Rec. 1610 (2003) on migration connected with trafficking in women and prostitution; Rec. 1663 (2004) on domestic slavery/ servitude, au pairs and mail-order brides and Resolution 1099 (1996) on the sexual exploitation of children.

The need for the CoE to reinforce its action in this field was underlined by the Foreign Affairs Ministers at the 112th (14–15 May 2003), 113th (5-6 November 2003) and 114th (12–13 May 2004) Sessions of the Committee of Ministers and on the occasion of the 5th European Ministerial Conference on Equality between Women and Man (Skopje, 22-23 January 2003). This led the CoE to launch the drafting of a Convention on Action Against Trafficking in Human Beings in September 2003 and a special web site devoted to this work was created: <www.coe.int/trafficking>.

During the 5th European Ministerial Conference on Equality between Women and Men, the CoE outlined three concrete objectives:

1. Promote equal opportunities, rights, freedoms and respect for women and men
2. Prevent and combat violence against women and trafficking in human beings
3. Develop gender mainstreaming within the council of Europe and at the national level.

Although activities to ensure the fulfilment of these objectives are separate from anti-trafficking activities, these activities should be seen as contributing to the fight against trafficking.

On May 16-17, 2005, during the 3rd Summitt of the CoE in Warsaw, the CoE Convention on Action Against Trafficking in Human Beings was opened for signature.

EUROPEAN UNION (EU)

EU Member States have undertaken actions to maximize cooperation in the fight against trafficking in human beings, and against trafficking in women and children in particular. Their anti-trafficking strategy identifies the root causes of trafficking as poverty, unemployment and lack of economic opportunities.

The European Parliament adopted a series of resolutions which include the protection of witnesses in the fight against organized crime, trafficking in human beings, and victims of violence who are minors.

The European Conference on trafficking in women for the purpose of sexual exploitation, held in Vienna in June 1996 and organized by the European Commission in collaboration with IOM, resulted in the Communication of the Commission to the Council and the European Parliament on this subject.[12] This document was later (1998) supplemented by a second Communication.[13] These texts focus on the need for national, regional and international cooperation and co-ordination between the authorities responsible for migration, justice and social affairs and NGOs. The Communications also asked for mutual cooperation between organizations such as the UN, the CoE, and the EU. This action was strengthened by the adoption of the Joint Actions of the Council based on Article K.3 of the European Union Treaty concerning action to combat trafficking in human beings and the sexual exploitation of children.

Two additional Communications were adopted in 2000[14] and 2003.[15] The 2000 Communication contains two Proposals for Council Framework Decisions on Combating Trafficking in Human Beings and on Combating the Sexual Exploitation of Children and Child Pornography. In June 2003, the European Commission adopted the Communication on the development of a common policy on illegal immigration, smuggling and trafficking of human beings, external borders and the return of illegal residents.

Several other declarations have been adopted by the EU; most important are the Hague and Brussels Declarations. The Hague Declaration contains guidelines for effective measures to prevent and combat trafficking in women for the purpose of sexual exploitation. The goal of the Brussels Declaration was to develop a mechanism for European and international cooperation and implementation of concrete measures, standards and best practices to combat trafficking in human beings.

Finally, the Council Framework Decision from 2000 contains provisions on state jurisdiction over crimes related to trafficking in human beings, on the introduction of penalties and on the protection of victims. The Framework Decision entered into force on August 1, 2002 and the EU Member States must implement it before August 1, 2004.

The EU has invested much effort in the development of a multi-disciplinary strategy to prevent trafficking. This strategy includes the STOP and DAPHNE programs and includes:

1. developing equivalent legislation in the EU and candidate countries;
2. collecting data and to provide research in field of gender studies;
3. improving prosecution of traffickers;
4. combating organized crime;
5. providing support and assistance for victims of trafficking.

THE STABILITY PACT FOR SOUTH EASTERN EUROPE

The Stability Pact for South Eastern Europe is a political agreement that was adopted at the Cologne Meeting of June 1999 as a European Union initiative. It was created by more than 40 Partner Countries and International Organizations with the aim of ensuring peace, democracy, respect for human rights, economic prosperity and stability throughout the region. In

September 2000, the Task Force on Trafficking in Human Beings was created, with the aim of fighting against trafficking through the promotion of training programs and the strengthening of national legislation on prevention, protection and assistance programs for the victims of trafficking.

THE SOUTHEAST EUROPEAN COOPERATION REGIONAL CENTER FOR COMBATING TRANS-BORDER CRIME (SECI)

The Southeast European Cooperative Initiative (SECI) with headquarters in Bucharest, Romania, supports efforts to fight trans-border crime in Southeast Europe with the main aim of improving the business environment in the region and making it attractive for investment. Its members are Albania, Bosnia and Herzegovina, Bulgaria, Greece, Croatia, Hungary, Macedonia, Moldova, Romania, Slovenia, and Turkey which all have police and customs officers assigned to the center in Bucharest. With its main objective of improving regional cooperation in combating trans-border crime through coordination efforts between law enforcement agencies of the participating states, SECI's work directly impacts efforts to combat trafficking of human beings.

UNITED STATES GOVERNMNET

The United States Government is involved in combating trafficking in human beings through the work of several agencies. In 2002, the U.S. Department of State set up an Office to Monitor and Combat Trafficking in Persons. The Office publishes an annual Trafficking in Persons Report (TIP), which presents anti-trafficking profiles for every country in the world and notes through a rating system how much effort the countries are making to combat trafficking in human beings.

The U.S. Department of Justice helps countries in the SEE region to combat trafficking in the region with its Resident Legal Advisor Program and through various assistance and training programs for law enforcement and judicial officials. The U.S. Federal Bureau of Investigation, whose mission includes responding to crimes against children, provides assistance with local anti-trafficking activities and training for international law enforcement agencies. USAID helps combat trafficking through grants to local organizations.

SUMMARY

Many international organizations are taking part in the fight against trafficking in human beings. Some of them strongly support strict standards for the implementation of legislative instruments, for example, international conventions that must be implemented by state parties. Others support "soft laws" such as resolutions, plans of action, and recommendations, the implementation of which depends on state decisions.

International organizations, on one side, and the countries of the world, on the other side, run at different speeds in the fight against this modern form of slavery. It is clear that state parties must be concerned not only with the implementation of international standards provided by the Trafficking Protocol and other treaties, but also with cooperation with NGOs, which have become important players in the fight against human trafficking. Unfortunately, in many transition countries, and in other countries as well, NGOs are not yet recognized by the government as partners in prohibiting trafficking; investigating, prosecuting, and punishing traffickers; and in protecting victims.

But, if they are to win the war on trafficking in human beings, governments need to work in close cooperation with NGOs and international organizations. They must recognize that this struggle requires a strong judicial commitment but also a firm commitment to assist trafficking victims whose human rights have been flagrantly violated.

Notes:

1. CEDAW, General Assembly Resolution 34/180, 18 December 1979.
2. CRC, General Assembly Resolution 44/25, 20 November 1989.
3. UN special reporter on violence against women, its causes and consequences (document E/CN.4/1977/47).
4. Nos. 29 and 105.
5. No. 182.
6. Conference for Security and Cooperation in Europe was replaced by OSCE in 1995.
7. *Human Dimension Commitments-A reference Guide*, (Warsaw: OSCE, 2001) 241.
8. Ibid. 299.
9, See: <http://www.osce.org/odihr/documents/trafficking/at-dec>.
10. See: < http://www.osce.org/odihr/documents/trafficking/at-dec>.
11. Permanent Council Decision No.426,PC.DEC/426,12 July 2001.
12. COM (96) 567 final.
13. COM (98) 726 final.
14. COM (2000) 0854 final.
15. COM (2003) 323 final.

Chapter 10

Migration and Human Trafficking in and around Southeast Europe

Migration is a natural phenomenon and often reflects people's simple wish for a better life, but it can also be the only alternative for survival, for example during war or conflict. Migration can be a simple process or one involving a series of steps. The first step may be moving from a rural to an urban area for the purpose of finding a job. The next step might be moving to another country that can be entered without problems, and where migrants can stay easily for either short or long periods of time. From these temporary transit countries, the process of migration may continue onward.

    Throughout history people have migrated and the ensuing problems created by this movement have provoked universal discussion and declaration about the rights of migrants. For example, the 1948 Universal Declaration of Human Rights (Article 13) states that: "...everyone has the right to leave any country, including his own." But the 1968 International Covenant on Civil and Political Rights (Article 12) sets limits by stating that these rights "shall be subject to restriction provided by law when required for national security, peace and public order, public health or moral, or the rights and freedom of others." So, although migration is acknowledged to be a basic human right, and the international legal order recognises the right to freedom of movement and residence, it is circumscribed by many qualifications and restrictions set by governments. For example, in some countries migrants may be accepted only if there is a demand for foreign labor,[1] in which case restrictions can be very flexible. There are also often special immigration privileges for nationals of certain states, people seeking reunification of family members, and, in some cases, individuals seeking political asylum or humanitarian protection that may be afforded to refugees. However, those people who do not qualify for legal migration may choose to continue their quest through illegal means and thus become "irregular migrants."

Since the early 1990s, conflict and economic hardship have made Southeast Europe a region of mass migration, and where there is mass migration, there is also irregular migration. Where there is irregular migration, there is smuggling of human beings, and where there is smuggling of human beings, trafficking in human beings and exploitation also exist. Irregular migration in and around Southeast Europe is mostly controlled by organized crime with an international network that covers the entire region and has strong ties to the border service, police, and border guards.

Much of the irregular migration is destined for Western Europe, which now recognizes this phenomenon, and irregular immigration has become a major issue in public debate. Western Europe is conflicted about how to deal with migrants. On the one hand, institutions such as the Council of Europe voice a human-rights approach to migration and it is logical that Europe would openly accept migrants, as European society is built on the contribution of migrants and Europe needs them.

But Western Europe, with its strict migration policy, continues to resist immigration flows, even though demographic trends suggest that even a significant increase in immigration will not by itself be able to meet future labor market demands. Yet people continue to migrate to Western Europe from all over the world. In fact, the European Union estimates that by the year 2023, 35 million people from Asia and Eastern Europe will have migrated to the European Union.

In terms of examining migration, one can view Southeast Europe as a point of origin and transit. There are four kinds of transitory people that can be found in Central, Eastern and Southeast Europe:

1. People who are moving throughout Central, Eastern and Southeast Europe, looking for economic betterment within one of the countries of the region. These people have often been classified as "tourists" because there have been no visa requirements for them.[2]

2. People who are using the countries of Central, Eastern, and Southeast Europe as a very temporary transit point en route to Western Europe, their ultimate destination. The high number of these transitory people has caused these regions to be labelled a "new migration space."

3. People moving within the regions of Central, Eastern and Southeast Europe and staying in one of the countries of these regions temporarily, but for a significant period of time. These people may later try to immigrate to Western Europe from one of these regions.

4. People who are moving due to war and political changes. The height of this transitory movement was between 1991 and 1997. For example, after the fall of the Soviet Union, over 10 million people voluntarily moved within Eastern

Europe. In addition, refugees fleeing from conflicts in the former Yugoslavia between 1990 and 1995 flooded the region: for instance, 80,000 of these refugees ended up in Hungary, for the most part in transit on their way to other places. And conflicts in the Caucasus – most significantly in Armenia, Azerbaijan and Chechnya – have caused a flow of approximately one million refugees into Russia.

Thus, hundreds of thousands of people have been on the move seeking a way out of economic hardship - many with the expectation of finding jobs in Western Europe. But the strict migration and asylum policies of Western European countries make it very difficult for citizens of Southeast Europe to enter the EU legally, which has created an opportunity for organized crime to step in and set up smuggling and trafficking enterprises. At the same time, many countries have had either weak or non-existent legislation penalizing people or organizations involved in smuggling or trafficking in human beings.

In this way, people in economically depressed countries such as Albania, Bulgaria, Romania, Moldova, and Ukraine were targeted from the very beginning. Criminal groups in Western Europe also recognized the opportunities created by these policies and made links with Southeast European crime groups for the purpose of organizing the sex trade in Western Europe. It is generally known that organized crime in Western Europe is composed of local criminals and criminal groups from Southeast Europe, comprised of the different ethnic groups of the region.

The following tables show a simplified scheme of migration flows and trafficking in human beings in Europe which illustrate the patterns of migration involving trafficking in women and children.

1. Within Central, Eastern, and Southeast Europe

From:	To:
Moldova	Romania, Czech Republic, Poland, Hungary, Serbia and Montenegro including Kosovo, Bosnia and Herzegovina, Macedonia, Albania
Ukraine	Czech Republic, Poland, Romania, Bulgaria, Serbia and Montenegro including Kosovo, Bosnia and Herzegovina, Macedonia, Albania
Romania (before the new visa regime for the EU)	Czech Republic, Hungary, Croatia, Slovenia, Slovakia, Serbia and Montenegro including Kosovo, Macedonia, Bulgaria, Albania, Bosnia and Herzegovina
Bulgaria (before the new visa regime for the EU)	Czech Republic, Romania, Macedonia, Serbia and Montenegro including Kosovo, Bosnia and Herzegovina, Albania
Serbia and Montenegro including Kosovo	Hungary, Croatia, Slovenia, Romania, Bosnia and Herzegovina, Macedonia, Albania
Macedonia	Albania, Turkey, Kosovo, Bulgaria, Croatia
Bosnia and Herzegovina	Serbia and Montenegro including Kosovo, Croatia
Croatia	Hungary, Slovenia, Serbia and Montenegro

2. Continuing from Central, East, and Southeast Europe
    into Western Europe[3]

From:	To:
Czech Republic, Slovakia, Slovenia, Hungary	Austria
Poland, Czech Republic	Germany
Albania, Macedonia, Bulgaria	Greece
Albania, Slovenia	Italy
Poland	Scandinavia

Standard migration system analysis is only partially useful for understanding migration which involves trafficking for the purpose of sexual exploitation. Patterson defines a migration system as "... any movement of persons between states, the social, economic and cultural effects of such movements and the patterned interactions among such effects."[4] Thus interactions between societies are created not only by flows of people but also by flows of information, services, goods and ideas.

So how does migration involving transnational trafficking fit into this system? According to the migration system approach, international migration flows should be seen as a result of the interaction between macro and microstructures. Macrostructures include the political economy of the world market and the laws and policies concerning migrants. Microstructures include social and informal networks and practices developed by migrants and their communities in order to cope with the consequences of migration.

On the macro level, one important factor that pushes women from Southeast Europe to immigrate to Western Europe is economic deprivation and domestic violence. However, micro-level analysis is not really applicable for female victims of transnational trafficking. They are isolated in conditions of slavery without the ability to contact other people, with the exception of customers. Their environment consists exclusively of women in the same position. These women do not interact with the rest of society until the moment they have contact with the police. Sometimes, if they are lucky enough to become a protected witness in the trial against a trafficker, which rarely happens, they may be able to stay in the country as a new immigrant. Only in these cases is it possible to speak about micro-level end interaction between these immigrants and society. As described in the previous chapters, women from Southeast and Central Europe are passive victims, which means that nobody takes into account the migration intentions and aims of the women. They are therefore marginalized as social actors, and, as a consequence, destination countries treat them as criminals rather than people who need help due to a cruel violation of their human rights.

The "structural theory" is rather different. In this view, the migrant is more like a ball in a pinball machine, knocked around by forces beyond his or her control. These forces could be economic or social or political nature, pushing people out of one country and pulling them towards another.

In the receiving country, the structural forces, which attract the immigrant, could be a shrinking population or a shortage of people to work as domestic servants. In these circumstances, the daughter of a landless Moldovan farmer might find it difficult to resist the forces "impelling" her to work in Kosovo or Italy. Therefore migration for the purpose of transnational trafficking should be regarded as a type of transnational labor migration and considered to be a special form of migration where a woman is exposed to violation, exploitation and humiliation without any right to make her own decisions.

Notes:

1. When the industrialized countries faced with labor shortages at times of full employment in the 1950s and 1960s, Europe did not hesitate to recruit workers from Turkey, the former Yugoslavia, Morocco, Algeria, India, Pakistan, etc. When the North and West were importing labor, the countries of the South and East encouraged their own people to migrate.
2. Migrants in groups 1 and 2 often have a valid international passport from their country of origin and move to a country that has no visa requirements as their first step in migration.
3. Once an irregular migrant who is a victim of trafficking finds herself/ himself in one of Western European countries, she/he can continue moving within these countries without any major problems.
4. O. Patterson, *Population in an Interacting World,* ed. W. Alonso (Cambridge: Harvard University Press, 1987) 227-62.

Chapter 11

Some Facts about
Sex Trafficking in Europe

Because there is currently no integrated and comprehensive system for collecting data on human trafficking, it is impossible to present definitive statistics and information. Instead, this chapter presents a sampling of information about forced prostitution and human trafficking in Europe – the available data show that Southeast and Eastern Europe have become the most important sources for prostitutes in Western Europe, trafficked or otherwise.

Interpol estimates that there are around 300,000 women from Southeast European countries engaged in prostitution in Western Europe[1] where they "live" and "work" in different conditions, including sexual slavery. The lack of complete data on migration, trafficking in women and children, or prostitution in Europe makes it impossible to precisely define the extent of the expansion in trafficking, but available data indicate that the phenomenon of trafficking in human beings is an increasing problem.

Vans used by prostitution rings serve as cheap hotel rooms

- In Germany, it is estimated that 75% of the prostitutes are originally from Southeast Europe or the countries of the former Soviet Union.[2] Russian women are the third-largest group of victims of trafficking in Germany, after Lithuanian and Ukrainian women.

- In Vienna, prostitutes from Eastern and Southeast Europe outnumber Austrian prostitutes by 5 to 1,[3] and approximately 80% of the "hostesses" and bar dancers in Vienna are from Eastern and Southeast Europe.

- In France, according to the Central Anti-Human-Trafficking Office, 12,000 to 15,000 people were engaged in prostitution in 2001.[4] In Nice, two out of three prostitutes are from Eastern Europe. Data also indicate that all Eastern European nationalities are involved: Romanian, Hungarian, Bulgarian, Czech, Croatian, Serb, Russian, Ukrainian, Slovak, Moldovan and Lithuanian women have worked as prostitutes in France since the early 1990s. Albanian women from Kosovo, Macedonia, and Albania joined them in 1997.

- In Italy, according to IOM data, 10-20% (2,000 to 6,000) of the 20,000 to 30,000 illegal female migrants who enter the sex industry each year are victims of trafficking. Albanian women are usually sold to Italy.[5]

- From Albania, between 1998 and 2003, more than 10,000 Albanian women and children were sold. An investigation in 1998 determined that at that time about 5,000 of the 14,000 Albanian women and girls living in Western Europe had been forced into prostitution and were living in conditions of sexual slavery. It is believed that up to 60% of victims from Albania are girls under the age of 18.[6]

- In the Czech Republic it is estimated that 20,000 women currently labor in sexual slavery.[7]

- In Greece, research has shown that over half of trafficked women and girls are from Russia and Ukraine, and one third of the women in the other half are from the Balkans.[8]

- In Belgium, data indicate that women are trafficked from Albania, Romania, Bulgaria and Russia, but also from Nigeria and Chile.[9]

- In the Netherlands, the majority of females trafficked are from Central and Eastern Europe.[10]

- Switzerland is also a destination country. The women who migrate into Switzerland usually come from Poland, Russia, Czech Republic, Lithuania and Albania.[11]

- According to IOM, Russian border guards between 1999-2000 intercepted 5,000 Russian women trying to leave the country with non-valid papers. The final destination for these women was Italy, Turkey, Germany, Finland, and also Bulgaria.[12]

- Belgrade, between 1999-2002 become the primary marketplace for the buying and selling of human beings in Southeast Europe. There are several marketplaces and also public auctions there. Buyers come from all over Europe and the Middle East to buy women in Belgrade. Prices for women range from US $1,000 to US $3000.[13]

EXAMPLES OF RESCUES OF TRAFFICKED WOMEN

- Paris, 2003 - Police broke up an Albania trafficking network that was preparing to force 10 Albanian women to work the Paris streets as prostitutes. The traffickers, an Albanian man and woman and a French man, had recently brought the women into France.[14]

- Brussels, 1999 - Police started running extensive document checks on the street, and found a significant number of juvenile prostitutes. Twenty-five of these girls, between 14 and 16 years old, had been trafficked from Bulgaria, Albania, and Ukraine.

- Spain, September 2002 - The police dismantled a network operating in a sex club in Bellvei, Tarragona, in which they detained twenty foreign women as well as the people in charge. Five of the women were Romanian, four Russian, three Belarussian, one Ukrainian and one Lithuanian; there were also women from Columbia, Brazil and Sierra Leone. The police also released a Russian citizen believed to have been kidnapped. They began the operation after receiving a report from Interpol in Moscow that a woman named Larisa had been kidnapped and forced against her will into sex work.[15]

- Belgrade, December 2000 - Yugoslav police arrested two men who, working with partners in Romania, allegedly organised the immigration of young women into Bosnia and Herzegovina, specifically into Republika Srpska. The daily newspaper *Politika* reported that police also found seventy women, mostly minors, from Moldova and Romania destined for illegal transfer to the Republika Srpska in order to work in bars. The price for transfer into Republika Srpska was 250 € for each woman.[16]

- Bosnia and Herzegovina, June 20, 2002 - In a raid on the bar "Roky" in Vitez (Canton Central Bosnia) five foreign women from countries of Southeast Europe were found to be victims of trafficking who had been forced into prostitution. In their statements given to the "STOP" team of the IPTF (International Police Task Force), these five women identified twenty-five policemen who were guests of the bar.[17]

EXAMPLES OF THE ARREST AND
PROSECUTION OF TRAFFICKERS

- Sheffield, Great Britain, 2005 - A 16 year old Lithuanian girl who was sold by Albanian criminals in Britain as a sex slave seven times in three months escaped after a mental breakdown in a Sheffield nightclub. A group of young English women distracted her Albanian minders long enough to allow her to run, barefoot and sobbing, to a nearby police station. Maka 24, Barjami 25, and Pisha 21, all Albanian asylum seekers, were subsequently convicted and imprisoned for 18, 15, and 7 years respectively. Two of their accomplices are now facing trial in Lithuania. The three now behind bars were the first in Britain to be charged under a law designed to halt the trafficking of women for sexual exploitation.[18]

- Spain, June 2001 - Sixty-nine people were arrested under charges of trafficking in women for purposes of prostitution. The international nature of trafficking can be seen in the

nationalities of the people arrested, which included two
Italians, a Lebanese, a Romanian, a Russian, a Pole, and
a Cuban. The criminal ring had both legal and illegal
enterprises: the legal enterprises included discos, bars, and
car sales.[19]

- Western Europe, October 2002 - Trans-border police raids
arrested 80 people for involvement in human trafficking.
Traffickers were arrested in Italy, Spain, Portugal, France,
Austria, Poland, Ukraine, Belarus, and Russia. The people
arrested included travel agents, managers of transportation
companies, and "hotel" owners. Police concluded that there
was close cooperation between Russian and Italian organized
crime groups in the trafficking of women and children.[20]

EXAMPLES OF ARREST AND DEPORTATION

- Italy, August 2002 - In an Italian police operation, 449
illegal immigrants were caught and many of them accused
of solicitation, pimping and dealing drugs. Deportation was
begun immediately. Police said that many of them were sent
home to Albania and other Balkan states.[21]

- France, Loiret, June 2001 - A Bulgarian trafficking network
as discovered and dismantled. The network was built by ten
people: eight from Bulgaria, one from France, and one from
Turkey. These ten people used two women to act as liaisons
with prostitutes from Southeast Europe who then ended up
as victims of trafficking. The traffickers were successfully
prosecuted and sentenced to five years imprisonment.
However, nine of them were deported instead of serving their
prison terms (the tenth man was French).[22]

Notes:

1. Parliamentary Assembly of the Council of Europe, DOC.9795, 25 April 2003.
2. S. Dusch, *Le traffic deters humains*. (Paris: Presse Universitaires de France, 2002) 47.
3. Dusch 148.
4. *Le Figaro*, 27 fevrier 2001.
5. *Trafficking in Migrants*, IOM, n°23, April 2001.
6. *Albanian Daily News*, 19 April 2001 and *World News Tonight*, 21 May 2001.
7. *Oslobodjenje*, 8 July 2001.
8. Dusch 157.
9. OIPC-Interpol, Assemblée Generale, Budapest, 24-28 September 2001.
10. Parliamentary Assembly of the Council of Europe, Doc. 9795, 25 April 2003.
11. Igor Davor Gaon, *Trafficking in Human Beings. Reflection Tables on Immigration and Human Rights*, (Athens, Council of Europe – Office of the Commissioner for Human Rights in cooperation with Marangopoulos Foundation for Human Rights, 5 April 2003).
12. *Trafficking in Migrants*, IOM, n°23, April 2001.
13. *[Stop-traffic] News/Balkans*, October 18, 2002.
14. *Prostitution et société*, juillet-septembre 2004.
15. See: <www.Lavanguardia.Es/web/20020912/31704229.html>.
16. *Agence France Presse*. December 5, 2000.
17. Published on ONASA web site, Sarajevo, 29 August 2002.
18. *News.Telegraph*, May 9, 2005. See: <http://news.telegraph.co.uk/news/main.jhtml?xml=/news/2005/05/09/nslave09.xml>.
19. *Prostitution et société*, July - September 2001.
20. *[Stop-traffic] News/Balkans*: October 18, 2002.
21. *The Associated Press*, August 14 2002.
22. *Prostititution et société*, October-December 2002.

PART II

Country Profiles

Introduction

In Part II, each chapter is devoted to a particular country, and follows the same pattern. The chapter begins with a checklist that tells you if the country is a source country, transit country, or destination country for human trafficking, and then gives a brief overview of the economic and social conditions which have led to the growth of human trafficking. Then, details are given about the trafficking methods and routes for the country, and the anti-trafficking laws and actions taken by the country's government. The chapter concludes with information about anti-trafficking action and victim assistance undertaken by NGOs and international organisations working in the country, as well as the government.

Because there is no regional standard for information collection and no regional data center for information on human trafficking, the data available for each country is far from comprehensive – data for one country may not be directly comparable with data for another country. This will unfortunately be the case until a plan for inter-regional communication and cooperation is designed and implemented in Southeast Europe.

Chapter 12

Albania

COUNTRY OF ORIGIN
COUNTRY OF TRANSIT
COUNTRY OF DESTINATION

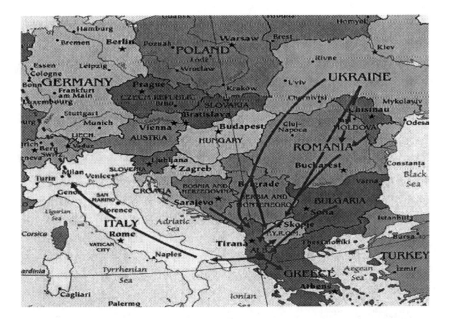

*An article in The Guardian reported the case
of a retired Italian couple who were arrested
for paying $6,000 to purchase a three-year-old
Albanian boy from an Albanian trafficking gang.
The boy had allegedly been traded by his father
for a color TV .*

Wsws. org., October 25, 2003

OVERVIEW

After the end of World War II, Albania became a communist state
under the leadership of Enver Hodza and was almost completely
isolated until its transition to democracy in the early 1990s.
The second half of the 1990s was politically unstable, with a
quick turnover of presidents and prime ministers. Particularly
disruptive was the 1997 collapse of country-wide pyramid
investment schemes, which sparked anti-government riots and
caused yet another change in government control.

Albanian mass migration began during Hodza's regime,
when many Albanians left the country to look for work: the
money sent home by émigrés has long been an important
source of revenue for Albania. The 1999 NATO bombing of
Yugoslavia brought 500,000 ethnic Albanian refugees from
Kosovo, and imposed an enormous burden on an already fragile
economy. At present, Albanians from rural areas, which are
characterized by poverty and high unemployment, are migrating
to cities and towns, and from cities and towns to search for
work outside of Albania. Young women are accustomed to
thinking of emigration as a standard option for finding work
or a financially secure husband – their willingness to emigrate
facilitates entrapment by human traffickers. There is a higher
rate of trafficking among rural women and girls, who are
often more naive than their counterparts in towns and cities.

The fragile and ineffective government, high number of refugees, and high level of unemployment and poverty have all contributed to the rise in the activity of gangs and other organized crime groups in Albania; these gangs and criminal organizations play a very important role in Albanian trafficking and forced prostitution. However, the government of Albania is making significant efforts to comply with international minimum standards for eliminating human trafficking.

In August 2002, the Government of Albania, working in cooperation with Italy, Greece, and Montenegro, organized a major air and sea operation against rampant smuggling gangs which had been using high-power launches for smuggling and human trafficking. Five speedboats were captured and at least 12 smugglers detained in Albanian's drive to round up gangs running migrants, sex slaves and drugs from the Albanian coast to Italy.[1] In a 2001 interview, one of these speedboat owners had confirmed that his net profit for one night's work could be as much as 10,000 €.[2]

Albanian officials, in response to pressure from the EU, have continued efforts to fight human trafficking focussing on organized crime operations, especially in the port region of Vlore.

ALBANIA AS A COUNTRY OF ORIGIN

Albanian women and girls, particularly those of rural origin, are mostly trafficked into Western Europe and also trafficked into other Balkan countries. Albanian pimps, working in conjunction with organized crime, run prostitution rings in many Western European cities – in particular, in southern Italy, London's Soho district, Frankfurt, Brussels, and Amsterdam. Albanian children are also trafficked to Greece. In 1997, Terre des Hommes reported that 400 children were sexually exploited in the Greek pedophile market of which 75% were Albanian, and 60% were male.

ALBANIA AS A TRANSIT COUNTRY

Albania is a common transit point for women who are trafficked from elsewhere in Southeast or Eastern Europe en route to Western Europe.

ALBANIA AS A DESTINATION COUNTRY

Some trafficked women, particularly from Ukraine, Moldova, Romania, Kosovo, Serbia, and Montenegro, remain in forced prostitution in Albania. Women who will fetch higher prices are often trafficked onward into Western Europe. Pimps and protectors, who usually have links to organized crime, operate prostitution rings in motels, hotels and bars. They also link up with drug dealers and traffickers to traffic women on into Western Europe.

Mirella's story illustrates the plight of Albanian girls who end up as trafficking victims.

Three years ago, 14 year old Mirella fell in love with an Albanian man. After several months, he proposed that they go to Belgium where they could earn a lot of money. She had no reason not to trust him - after all, from her point of view, they had been together for a long time.

They left for Italy by speedboat from Vlore and traveled by car to Milan from where they easily reached Belgium. Upon arrival, her boyfriend supplied her with a Greek passport that stated she was 18, and informed her that she would have to work as a prostitute. He told her that her assignment was to bring in 500 € per night. The first night when she brought in only 200 €, he was unsatisfied and beat her.

As time went by, he was more and more

vicious. Finally she couldn't stand it anymore, went to the police, and told them her story. The pimp was arrested and sentenced to a few months in prison. Upon his release, he set out to kill Mirella. His threat was clear: "If I am not able to find her, I will seek revenge on her family." Now Mirella is in the care of a Belgium NGO, but her pimp is still looking her.

SOME PROSTITUTION AND TRAFFICKING STATISTICS

In 1997, IOM reported that approximately 50,000 Albanian women had been trafficked into Italian brothels in the previous two years.[3] In 1998, several reports were published by different human rights groups. According to one of these reports, more than 14,000 Albanian women and girls were working as prostitutes in several European countries. Another group reported that there were 8,000 Albanian women and girls working as prostitutes in Italy (30% of them were minors), approximately 5,000 in Greece, 250 in Austria, and 180 in France; Albanian women have also been found in Britain, Germany and Switzerland. The study indicated that organized crime groups from Albania do not hesitate to use violence to control these women and girls.[4]

According to some Albanian NGOs, 30,000 Albanian women work as prostitutes and are victims of trafficking in Europe: 15,000 in Italy, 6,000 in Greece and the rest in other European countries. An independent commission investigating trafficking has found 97 cases of trafficking since 1995, with 90% of the victims under the age of 18. This commission found that 63% of Albanian women and girls ended up in Italy, 18% in Greece, and 16% in Belgium. In the Berat district of Albania, they found that approximately 2,000 women and girls are living abroad, and that at the time of their departure, 80% of them had been minors. In the city of Koçova, 650 young women have been the victims of trafficking.[5]

In 1999, UNICEF reported that Albanian gangs were kidnapping refugee girls from Kosovo and trafficking them to brothels in Italy.[6] In 2000, Italian police arrested 69 Albanians involved in the organization of prostitution and trafficking of drugs. More than 600 policemen were involved in the operation in south and central Italy.[7] One year later, Italian police arrested more then 100 men suspected of trafficking in human beings; most of them were Albanian. The police indicated that these men had forced hundreds of young women from Albania, Southeast Europe and South America into prostitution.[8] A report by Daniel Renton states that approximately 40% of Albanian prostitutes in Italy are minors.[9]

Perhaps the most realistic picture can be found in the document "National Strategy to Combat Trafficking in Human Beings," prepared by the Council of Ministers in Tirana in 2001. This document states that in the last 10 years, around 100,000 Albanian women and girls have been trafficked into Western Europe and Balkan countries.[10] According to the government figures, 437 women were repatriated to Albania in 2000 and 2001. Forty percent of these women stated that they had been forced into prostitution.[11] In addition, according to the Albanian Ministry of Labor and Social Affairs there are at least 6,000 Albanian children in Italian orphanages and 1,000 to 2,000 children in Greek orphanages.[12]

IOM has assisted trafficking victims in Albania with shelter and repatriation: the majority of the trafficked girls and women were from Moldova and Romania. In 2000, IOM/ICMC provided assistance to 125 women and girls; 13% of them were under 18. From January to November of 2001, IOM assisted another 60 foreign women and girls who were victims of trafficking.[13] According to the Albanian police, in 2002 there were only 12 cases of foreign women being trafficked. In 2002, the Vatra Shelter for trafficked victims in Vlora reported assisting 13 foreigners.

The Italian ministry of the interior reported in 2001 that 168 foreign prostitutes had been murdered, mainly by their pimps. The majority of the murdered women were either Albanian or Nigerian.[14]

> *When she was 12, "Irina" left home and went with her boyfriend to Greece. There she worked as a prostitute together with her mother and sister-in-law and became pregnant.When her child was born, her boyfriend sold the baby for 1000 €. After this happened, she escaped and returned to Albania where she found a new boyfriend who took her to Italy to work the streets. As her pimp, he forced her to work night and day until she had a complete mental collapse. Now, still not 18, she is in Italy in a psychiatric hospital.*

Albanian pimps also organize prostitution in France, but often remain based in Germany and Belgium while managing smaller criminals who live with the women and control them. Usually these smaller criminals are the ones who are arrested and serve time while the "big fish" remain out of reach. [15]

Albanian criminals in Britain have organized modern sex slavery and an entire underworld regime financed by the rich profits of prostitution. Their strong network connections make it possible to bring women into Britain from Russia, the Baltic States, Romania, Moldova or the Balkans.[16] Scotland Yard's Vice Squad estimates that 70% of off-street sex services in Soho – brothels, saunas and massage parlors – are run by foreigners, including gang members from countries such as Albania.[17]

> *Ivana, a citizen of Ukraine, was kidnapped by a gang of human traffickers and trafficked around Europe for six months. She was trafficked into Macedonia and then to*

*Greece, where she was sold to an Albanian man
who took her to the UK via Italy. Ivana ended
up as a victim of trafficking in Birmingham,
England.*

> *"The first time he raped me, I fought him
> for half an hour – but he was a massive man, and
> I am quite small. He was really crazy. He beat me
> all the time even out in the street – with his hands,
> his feet, his belt - my body was all black and blue.
> He used to make me work every day – even when
> I had my period. I used to see six, seven, or even
> more customers a day. I was thinking of suicide
> by throwing myself out the window of the brothel,
> but when the cleaning lady saw how sad I was,
> she and two other prostitutes carried me into her
> car and helped me escape." Now Ivana lives in
> fear that her pimp will find her. If he does, she
> believes he will kill her.[18]*

According to UNICEF's 2003 report *Trafficking In Human
Beings In Southeastern Europe*, by Barbara Limanowska, the
situation in illegal migration and trafficking from Albania is
improving as the government has taken a number of serious
initiatives to combat illegal migration and trafficking. The report
states that in 2002, the number of women trafficked from and
returned to Albania significantly declined. The Albanian police
put this number at zero, since they have shut down the main
trafficking routes. However, some dispute this.[19] According to
Albanian NGOs, trafficking and transiting of women through
Albania still exists but on a smaller scale.

One could conclude from these declining numbers that
the transit routes are in fact closed. On the other hand, it is also
possible that traffickers have found new crime strategies for
their business that affects the statistics. Local NGOs in Albania
have noted that the number of foreign women working in bars
and hotels has recently increased and this corresponds with

information that organized crime is investing in hotels, bars, and other businesses. According to the ILO, Albania, Moldova, and Ukraine are still important sources of trafficked women. Gail Kligman, Professor of Sociology and Director Designate for the Center of European and EuroAsian Studies at the University of California at Los Angeles supports this conclusion in a report published in March 2005, "Trafficking of Women After Socialism: From, To and Thru Eastern Europe."[20]

TRAFFICKING METHODS AND ROUTES

The main trafficking routes into Albania are:
- Eastern countries > Moldova > Romania > Serbia > Macedonia > Albania
- Serbia > Kosovo > Macedonia > Albania
- Serbia > Montenegro > Albania

The main trafficking routes out of Albania are:
- Albania > Greece (by land)
- Albania > Italy (by sea, usually via the ports of Durres or Vlora – although the police have stated that these routes no longer exist)

There are many markets in Albania for buying and selling women. The main markets are in Shkodra and Malesi for women trafficked in via Montenegro, and in Korca for women trafficked in via Macedonia. Smaller markets can also be found in Nerat, Elbasan, Laç, Fier, and Tirana.

ACTIONS AND LAWS AGAINST TRAFFICKING

Actions

The government went after traffickers with its Organized Crime Task Force, which is made up of special police and prosecutors. Though the borders remain porous, interdiction at Albania's main entry and exit ports has improved. In Vlora, an anti-trafficking center (VATC) has been opened to gather information and create regional anti-trafficking responses.[21]

In the absence of regular police anti-trafficking action, Albanians sometimes resort to vigilante justice: some families in rural regions who have had family members trafficked into prostitution have killed the traffickers responsible.

Laws and Prosecution

Prostitution is illegal in Albania, and the Criminal Code of Albania also prohibits trafficking and provides for a penalty of up to 15 years imprisonment. In the case of trafficking in minors the penalty is between 15 and 25 years imprisonment. In 2003, the Albanian government arrested 317 people for crimes related to trafficking, received 102 convictions, and imposed 75 sentences of two to ten years' imprisonment.

PROBLEMS

A major problem fighting human trafficking in Albania is police corruption: it has been reported that 10% of foreign victims who were trafficked through Albania claimed that the police were directly involved in their trafficking.[22] According to the Albanian Interior Ministry, during the first five months of 2002, 102 officers were identified as being involved in the trafficking of women and girls. Sixteen of the suspects were jailed, 12 were transferred to other jobs and 15 received minor punishment.

Although in the past, trafficking victims were routinely treated as criminals, the police now regularly refer them to NGOs for victim assistance. While there are temporary shelters for trafficking victims who will be serving as witnesses for prosecution, there is no comprehensive program for witness protection.

The Albanian Government is investing time and resources to combat organized crime, especially relating to trafficking in human beings since Albanian organized crime outside of the country, mostly in Western Europe, is generating problems inside the country. The Albanian mafia in Western Europe is using Albania as a bridge for trafficking human beings and drugs from the East to the West. In June 2003, the World Markets Research Centre reported that Albanian mafia groups have established a reputation in continental Europe as being among the most efficient drug pushers and smugglers of people on the continent. For instance, the Albanian mafia is very active in Germany – it is involved with trafficking of drugs and people, establishing new rules of prostitution, and pushing the Turkish mafia out of business.[23]

The Albanian mafia has begun to dominate the drug and paid sex markets in Italy as well. The Albanian Cartel in Milan controls prostitution there, where people new to the business must pay for space to work. This cartel controls the marketplace for women from Southeast Europe, where the price for young girls can be as high as 10,000 €. Italian officials estimate that 16.6% of women and girls working as sex slaves in Italy are from Ukraine, 50% from Romania, 12% from Moldova and 7% from Albania.[24]

A young Albanian woman was kidnapped by her neighbour, and ended up on the streets of a Belgian city. At the time she went missing, her younger sister "M" went to the police and gave

*the names of the two people who had kidnapped
her sister. The kidnappers immediately got word
that "M" had been to the police and went to her
home where they attacked her younger brother,
telling him that in case the family continued with
action against them, they would also kidnap "M"
and force her into prostitution. But when "M's"
father arrived on the scene, it was already too
late - the room was full of blood and "M" had
disappeared. Later they found her body close to
the river. The criminals were arrested - but for
drug trafficking. The family never reported the
disappearance of "M" because they were terrified
of the criminals and didn't trust the police.*

WORK BY NGOS AND INTERNATIONAL ORGANIZATIONS

In 2002, IOM began helping Albanian women who had been
trafficked; they opened a shelter in Tirana, and began a program
of long-term assistance in reintegration that includes training
and support in finding jobs. They also have a shelter in Vlora
managed by a local NGO, Vatra.

Another organization, Vlora Women's Health, located in
Vlora, assists trafficked Albanian women who have been deported
from Italy. The international NGO Terre des Hommes (TdH) and
a local NGO Help for Children (NPF) are jointly implementing
a prevention project for children and their families. Since 2002,
TDH in collaboration with UNICEF has been developing a
project to combat trafficking of children.

*Namik Shehaj, who runs a UNICEF-
funded child protection project in Albania, says
that parents sometimes sell their children out of
desperation. "Actually, the parents send the kids
to Greece because they see it as a possibility to*

*earn money. And this is a contagious disease,
because you see your neighbor - he has sent his
kid to Greece - he has gone there himself even.
So you ask yourself, 'Why shouldn't I send mine?'
The only reason these children are trafficked and
exploited is the poor economic situation of the
family."*[25]

Advocates for children say well-organized criminal gangs are taking advantage of poor families and offer them small amounts of money to buy their children. In many of these cases, young girls end up in the sex trade. Fifteen-year-old Yasmina, a girl rescued by Mr. Shehaj's organization, was originally sold to work as a street beggar. Later, she was forced into prostitution. "I was four years old, too small. I was with a neighbor. He gave some money to my father and then took me there, to Greece. My neighbor gave my father 25,000 leke ($253), so it was like my father sold me."[26]

International Social Service (ISS), is working on the return of children under 18 from Italy. In 2002, the organizations working on child trafficking formed a coalition, "All Together Against Child Trafficking" (BKTF). Other IOs and NGOs with operations in Albania are IOM, ICMC, UNHCR, and OSCE. However, the majority of trafficked Albanian women do not receive support or assistance with reintegration.

Notes:

1. *Reuters,* 21 August 2002.
2. H. Bokhorest, *Femmes dans les Griffes des Aigles* (Bruxelles:Editions

Labor, 2003).

3. *Report on Trafficking, International Organization for Migration*, 1997.

4. *Agence France Press*, 18 July 1998.

5. Bokhorst.

6. *Miami Herald*, 30 May 1999.

7. *Albanian Daily News*, 21 June 2000.

8. *BBC*, 9 April 2000.

9. D. Renton, *Child Trafficking in Albania*, (Tirana: Save the Children, 2000) 9.

10. *A National Strategy to Combat Trafficking in Human Beings*: Page 12.

11. Ibid., p.15.

12. Government Conference on Trafficking; "All Together Against Child Trafficking," Presentation of the Ministry of Labor and Social Affairs, Tirana, November 2001.

13. Barbara Limanowska, *Trafficking In Human Beings in Southeastern Europe*, (Belgrade: UNICEF, UNOHCHR, OSCE/ODIHR, 2002) 127.

14. *Balkan Crisis Report*, Institute for Women's Policy Research (IWPR), No. 460, 15 September 2003.

15. *Le Figaro*, 1 October 2002.

16. *Yorkshire Post*, 16 July 2002.

17. *The Guardian*, 26 March 2003.

18. *BBC NEWS*, 3 November 2004. For the full story, see: <http://news.bbc.co.uk/2/hi/europe/3979725.stm>.

19. Barbara Limanowska, *Trafficking In Human Beings in South Eastern Europe*, (Belgrade: UNICEF, UNOHCHR, OSCE/ODIHR, 2003) 35.

20. *Trafficking of Women After Socialism: From, To and Thru Eastern Europe*, East European Studies Meeting Report No. 312, March 11 2005.

21. *Victims of Trafficking and Violence Protection Act of 2000: Trafficking in Persons Report*, (Washington, D.C., U.S. Department of State, 2004).

22. *Victims of Trafficking and Violence Protection Act of 2000: Trafficking in Persons Report*, (Washington, D.C., U.S. Department of State, 2001).

23. *Le Figaro*, 1 October 2002.

24. *ANSA.it-news in English*, 28 July 2005.

25. *VOA News*, 25 May 2005. See: <http://author.voanews.com/english/2005-05-25-voa60.cfm>

26. Ibid.

Chapter 13

Bosnia and Herzegovina

COUNTRY OF ORIGIN
COUNTRY OF TRANSIT
COUNTRY OF DESTINATION

Overview

The Dayton Agreement, signed in November 1995, ended the war in the West Balkans and established Bosnia and Herzegovina as a state with an unusual and specific structure. The agreement retained Bosnia and Herzegovina's international boundaries and created a government led by a multi-ethnic Council of Ministers (the State Government). The agreement dictated that the State should be divided into two entities, the Federation of Bosnia and Herzegovina and Republika Srpska. These distinct entities would operate as the second level of government with each functioning as a state with its own army, police, etc. Dayton also divided the Federation of Bosnian and Herzegovina into 10 cantons, thus setting up the third level of government. The treaty also established the Office of the High Representative (OHR) to oversee the implementation of civilian aspects of the agreement. Subsequently, international arbitrage established District Brcko, which functions as a state within the state.

Since, at the time the treaty was signed, Bosnia and Herzegovina did not have a unified police force, state border control or uniform customs control, international organizations were assigned the task of supervising the implementation of laws and ensuring human rights standards. The result was that tens of thousands of foreigners settled in Bosnia and Herzegovina including approximately 60,000 foreign soldiers assigned to insure the peace. For organized crime, which had established itself during the war, and for that element of the political elite linked to organized crime, the Dayton Agreement, which should have brought peace and stability to the country, presented a perfect opportunity to maintain their established criminal businesses and to develop a new one, namely, trafficking in human beings for the purpose of sexual exploitation.

Within a short time Bosnia and Herzegovina was overrun with nightclubs and bars which served as fronts for both voluntary and forced prostitution. International organizations based in

Bosnia and Herzegovina have been officially concerned with the problem of human trafficking since their first conference on the matter in 1998, which laid the foundation for projects to combat human trafficking in Southeast Europe.

In June 2003, a report by the U.S. State Department identified Bosnia and Herzegovina as a "Tier 3" country, that is, a country that does not meet the minimum standards for fighting trafficking in human beings. But Bosnia and Herzegovina's Council of Ministers (the State Government) reacted immediately by strengthening its law enforcement response and with anti-corruption measures. In September 2003, the State Department responded to these actions by changing the ranking to "Tier 2."

BOSNIA AND HERZEGOVINA AS A COUNTRY OF ORIGIN

In the meantime, the State Government has taken over border control of Bosnia and Herzegovina and many foreign peacekeepers have left the country. Thus it has become a less attractive destination for traffickers bringing in women and girls from abroad. However, according to local NGOs in Bosnia and Herzegovina, since 2004, domestic pimps have been focussing on local women and girls and trafficking them throughout the country and abroad.

BOSNIA AND HERZEGOVINA AS A COUNTRY OF TRANSIT

Women trafficked to Western Europe via Bosnia and Herzegovina travel on these routes:
- Countries of origin > Serbia > Bosnia and Herzegovina > Montenegro > Albania > Western Europe
- Bosnia and Herzegovina > Croatia > Western Europe
- Border crossings into Serbia are often from Hungary, Romania or Bulgaria

BOSNIA AND HERZEGOVINA AS A COUNTRY OF DESTINATION

Following the end of the war in Bosnia and Herzegovina in 1995, the country was flooded with thousands of peacekeepers and became a prime destination for traffickers of women and girls from Moldova, Romania, Ukraine, and elsewhere in the former Yugoslavia. Many of them were trafficked into Bosnia and Herzegovina via Serbia. As the peacekeepers have left the country, however, Bosnia and Herzegovina has become a less attractive destination for traffickers.

SOME PROSTITUTION AND TRAFFICKING STATISTICS

Between March 1999 and March 2000, 182 victims of trafficking were assisted in Bosnia and Herzegovina. Of these victims, 64 were from Moldova, 60 were from Romania, 37 were from Ukraine, 9 were from Croatia, 2 were from Bosnia and Herzegovina, 2 were from Kazakhstan, and one was of unknown origin. Five of these victims were under the age of 18, and 62 of them returned voluntarily to their home countries.[2]

On October 30, 2000, 12 victims of trafficking were discovered during a police raid on a nightclub in Sarajevo.[3] As of July 2001, IOM had rescued and repatriated 329 women and girls who had been trafficked for the purpose of sexual exploitation. IOM also reported that 25% of the women working in bars and nightclubs in Bosnia and Herzegovina claim to have been forced into prostitution. Ten percent of these were girls under the age of 18 years.[4]

In March 2001, police raided 38 brothels throughout Bosnia and Herzegovina, arresting 223 people involved in prostitution and trafficking. The majority of the women who were detained were from Romania, Moldova, Ukraine and Russia.[5]

In November 2001, UN officers raided several night bars in the town of Prijedor (in the northwest part of Bosnia and Herzegovina) and rescued 37 women working as prostitutes, the majority were from Romania and Moldova. However, following the raids the bars were not closed, and the owners of the bars were not prosecuted.[6]

From its formation in July 2001, the UN's International Police Task Force ran the Special Trafficking Operations Program (STOP), a task force led by international officers, whose mission was to combat trafficking in women. STOP raided 667 premises in Bosnia and Herzegovina, and assisted 196 of 1,997 women interviewed – implying that only 10% were trafficked against their will.[7] On June 8, 2002, STOP raided more than 213 suspect establishments throughout the country, closing 116 of them.[8]

In a progress review of STOP presented in Sarajevo on August 1, 2002, one year after it was launched, officials said that UN and Bosnian police had conducted 600 raids on some 200 bars and clubs suspected of using trafficked woman for prostitution, and that 182 women, mostly from Romania, Ukraine and Moldova, were helped to return to their countries. In 2002, STOP found and interviewed 1,847 women who were potential victims of trafficking.[9]

In September 2002, an intensive European operation was organized, with American assistance, to crack down on trafficking in women for the sex trade. The operation in Central and Southeast Europe had mixed success, and American officials suggested that in fact little was done in Bosnia and Herzegovina. National and international police officers made 71 raids on nightclubs, hotels and other locations during the September operation, but arrested only seven trafficking suspects.[10]

Estimates on the numbers of bars and nightclubs suspected in involvement in prostitution varied greatly: the UNMIBH claimed that they numbered 260, while local NGOs claimed that the number of bars was more like 900, with between 4 and 25 women in each bar and nightclub. However, there are no consistent figures available.

In January 2003, local police raided 47 nightclubs under the close watch of the EU Police Mission to Bosnia and

Herzegovina (EUMP). Since January 1, 2003 when it took over from the UN's 1600-strong international police force (UNMIBH), EUMP has assumed a monitoring role. About 500 higher-level EUMP managers are at 43 locations around Bosnia and Herzegovina to monitor the police. Two hundred police officers from Bosnia and Herzegovina were involved in the January raid, and the result was that one night-bar in Tuzla was closed, one woman victim of trafficking in Bijeljina was brought into a shelter, and, in Travnik, police found three women who had entered Bosnia and Herzegovina without documents.[11]

In 2003, modern slave owners in Bosnia and Herzegovina started to promote a new "technology" using private apartments to offer girls' and women's services through phone calls. This new trend of "hotlines" allows traffickers to remain hidden, while victims are still forced to engage in sex work.[12]

The dramatic increase in the number of women trafficked to and from Bosnia and Herzegovina can be traced directly to the arrival of peacekeepers in Bosnia and Herzegovina. Many reports have indicated that the UN covered up the involvement of UN police task forces in human trafficking[13]. The UN did, however, dismiss an American officer for procuring a Moldovan woman for prostitution in a brothel in Sarajevo for the sum of $2, 900.[14]

Several reports have suggested that local police have been involved in either protecting or just overlooking the illegality of brothels in Bosnia and Herzegovina. Some of these claims can be found in the Human Rights Watch report *Trafficking of Women and Girls to Post-Conflict Bosnia and Herzegovina for Forced Prostitution.* For example, several cases are documented where chiefs of local police stations were guests of brothels free of charge, or where police officers were directly involved in trafficking.[15]

Since 2003, there has been evidence of some improvement in trafficking and in the treatment of women in prostitution. Some data indicate that the owners of bars and nightclubs are now paying and treating the women better, and that they are not as likely to be held in slave-like conditions. Women are more likely to report that they are working voluntarily and have not been trafficked. Some sources state they are paid, although still underpaid and obliged to pay for their room and meals.

Yet, the story of Olena told at the beginning of this book, illustrates how serious the situation remains. In another case, Ina, a Moldovan citizen, came to a police station near Zenica to file a complaint that she had been forced into prostitution by a Moldovan woman, a colleague who was also a "coordinator" for East European prostitutes. This woman was arrested but 24 hours later was allowed to go free while the investigation continues.[16]

> *A new case reported in "Dnevni Avaz" on April 13, 2005, reveals that the State Agency for Investigation and Protection (SIPA) with the assistance of the Special Unit of the Department for Crime of the Canton arrested 3 men from Mostar and charged them with trafficking for the purpose of sexual exploitation. The arrest was made based on the accusation of a victim of trafficking from the State Union of Serbia and Montenegro. The accusations included trafficking, pimping and sexual slavery. The victim who is prepared to give testimony is now under police protection.*

In July 2005, *AIM-NG News* reported that two individuals from Banja Luka were sentenced for trafficking in human beings for sexual exploitation. They had been arrested after having forced a girl from Bijeljina to provide sex services from February 2003 to November 2004 to pay the rent for her apartment. The story also reported that seven other people from Bijelna are under investigation for trafficking in human beings for sexual exploitation from Serbia to Bosnia and Herzegovina.

TRAFFICKING METHODS AND ROUTES

Women and girls from other countries who end up in Bosnia and Herzegovina are first trafficked into Serbia, and from there into Bosnia and Herzegovina. Common border crossings are used by traffickers are Bijeljina and Zvornik.

ACTIONS AND LAWS AGAINST TRAFFICKING

Actions

In November 2000, under the leadership of the Ministry for European Integration, the National Working Group on Trafficking was established. This working group is designed to identify anti-trafficking priorities, and coordinate action on the part of the government, NGOs, and international organizations. Then, in December 2000, Bosnia and Herzegovina signed two international documents on combating the trafficking of human beings. In December 2001, the Council of Ministers adopted the National Plan of Action developed by the working group. Its areas of focus include:

- a committee responsible for implementation of the NPA
- budgets and funding for implementation of the NPA
- border control and law enforcement
- victim assistance and support (e.g., through building of shelters)
- legal reform, in particular standardization of legal codes throughout the Federation
- education and information campaigns.

In addition, there have been coordinated police raids. For example, in March 2001, police raided 39 bars in one night in operation "Macro."[17] Police found 177 foreign women in the raided bars; they referred 13 of these women to IOM, but also arrested 42 women (34 foreign, 8 from Bosnia and Herzegovina) on charges of prostitution – these women were fined or jailed or deported. It is not clear how many of the women who were arrested were also victims of trafficking. The police of Bosnia and Herzegovina are currently being trained in protocols for dealing with victims of trafficking, and how to cooperate with IPTF.

In March 2002, the Council of Ministers established a state commission to oversee implementation of the NPA, but by mid-2003 little had been accomplished by this body. In July 2003, a new National Coordinator was finally appointed.

According to the U.S. State Department 2005 Trafficking in Persons Report, the Government of Bosnia and Herzegovina has increased its capacity to prevent and respond to incidents of corruption and is now investigating cases of official complicity in trafficking. In October 2004, a police officer was arrested for trying to traffic two victims at the border with Serbia and Montenegro and was suspended from duty, indicted, and now is awaiting trial.[18]

Laws and Prosecution

The State Government of Bosnia and Herzegovina is improving its law enforcement response and anti-corruption efforts in relation to trafficking. In 2004, the police investigated and gave prosecutors 47 cases and the courts handed down 18 verdicts with 12 convictions. However, punishments tended to be light – one year or less – even though Bosnia and Herzegovina's criminal code provides for up to 10 years imprisonment for trafficking related crimes.[19]

Much depends on individual judges and both their comprehension of the problem of human trafficking and their interpretation of the law. In Bosnia and Herzegovina, traffickers can be prosecuted for the following criminal offenses: slave-holding and transport of human beings in slavery, kidnapping, deprivation of freedom, rape, sexual intercourse with minors, and assisting in prostitution. In Republika Srpska, traffickers can be prosecuted for the following criminal offenses: coercive pregnancy termination, serious bodily injuries, deprivation of freedoms, kidnapping, illegal deprivation of freedoms, sexual abuse of children, trafficking in persons for the purposes of the prostitution (Article 188).

In March 2003, the Office of the High Representative (OHR) imposed a new Criminal Code of Bosnia and Herzegovina. The Code imposes a penalty of 1-10 years imprisonment for trafficking in human beings. For the trafficking of a "minor," the minimum penalty is 5 years, but the article does not define the age of a minor. For international recruitment, the penalty is from 6 months to 5 years; for slavery and transportation of enslaved persons, 1-10 years; and for cases involving juveniles or deprivation of documents a minimum of 5 years.

PROBLEMS

Prosecution is misguided and often has the wrong result. Rather than focus on the actual criminal, the trafficker, prosecutors focus on the victims, who are often denied translation help or legal advice. In the late 1990s, the implementation of "expulsion" from one canton to another actually helped traffickers in their recycling and reselling of women from one brothel to another. However, this deportation stopped in 1999, and trafficked women are now referred to IOM and its victim assistance services.

Law enforcement in Bosnia and Herzegovina is spotty, and police have often turned a blind eye to trafficking, for example, when they issue work permits to bar owners for "dancers" and "waitresses," even though it is clear that these women are actually working as prostitutes. People in law enforcement are themselves sometimes involved in trafficking – military forces and police can be clients of trafficked women forced to work as prostitutes,[20] and some local police have been implicated as themselves being traffickers.[21]

In 2003, according to Sven Frederickson, Commissioner of the EU Police Mission in Bosnia and Herzegovina, this police and military involvement appeared to be waning. He gave a less ominous picture of human trafficking in an interview in the daily newspaper *Dnevni Avaz*. Commissioner Frederickson noted that there were no policemen that had been charged with trafficking. According to Frederickson, between January and June of 2003, just 29 people were prosecuted for trafficking, 15 people were charged with prostitution, and 34 of the 350 women interviewed with regard to their work as prostitutes asked for help. He also took issue with the numbers found in the University of Lozano Report on prostitution in Bosnia and Herzegovina, which noted that approximately 15,000 prostitutes were at the time working in the country; Frederickson claimed that the number was closer to 210 women.[22]

According to local NGOs, 40 percent of the clients in BiH are foreigners, mainly soldiers from SFOR. The EUPM puts this number at 30%. However, the situation is changing because the number of foreign soldiers is decreasing from more than 60,000 in 1996 to some 12,000 in 2003. But the NGO community does not see a decline in the sex market and anticipates that local demand will simply replace the demand of international clients. The Ministry of the Interior of the Republika Srpska (RS) is more optimistic since their numbers are steadily declining. In 2003, there were 8 nightclubs in RS employing 23 women, down from 70 bars with 470 women in 2001.

On June 7, 2005, officials of the Ministry of Interior Affairs of the Federation of Bosnia and Herzegovina, in an action initiated by the Office of the Prosecutor of the State of Bosnia and Herzegovia, closed the night club Mlin near Zivince in Tuzla Canton after the discovery of six foreign women who were victims of trafficking. Four people were arrested and they are under investigation. Recently 12 bars in Tuzla Canton have been closed for prostitution. In two of the bars, the Mlin and Mona Liza, officials found foreign trafficking victims. In the other bars, the prostitutes were all of domestic origin.[23] *The Bosnia Daily* reported on July 26, 2005, that NGOs in Bosnia and Herzegovina dealing with the sex trade say they have recently detected an increasing number of local women and girls falling into the trap of human trafficking.[24]

The government has developed a protocol on the protection of foreign victims of trafficking which includes the issuing of humanitarian visas. Prosecutors may request such visas and victims may be protected and housed in shelters. But the government did not implement a screening system, so some victims were not identified and were thus denied proper protection and ordered out of the country. Often, however, such orders for deportation were not enforced and the victims fell back into the hands of traffickers. Bosnia and Herzegovina also needs to develop and adopt legislation regarding assistance to domestic victims of trafficking.[25]

WORK BY NGOS AND INTERNATIONAL ORGANIZATIONS

INTERNATIONAL ORGANIZATIONS

- Since 1998, UNHCHR has been a leader in awareness-raising on the topic of human trafficking.
- Despite the formation of a National Plan of Action by the government, most victims of human trafficking were assisted by UNMIBH and IPTF until the beginning of 2003 when The European Union Police Mission (EUPM) took over some of the IPTF's functions.
- IOM gives full assistance to victims of trafficking. In 2001, IOM assisted 200 women; in 2002, 255 women; and in the first 6 months of 2003, 17 women.
- The OSCE Mission to Bosnia and Herzegovina is working

with the International Human Rights Law Group to implement two projects for the legal protection of trafficked women and children.

- La Strada began giving assistance to trafficking victims in January 2002.
- International Forum of Solidarity (IFS) started providing assistance in 2002.
- Since 2002, IOM has provided assistance to 21 domestic victims of trafficking of which 14 were in 2004.[26]

NGOs

- Several local NGOs have been actively providing assistance for victims of human trafficking for years.
- In 1999, local NGOs formed a coalition called "The Ring," which has developed its own Action Plan.
- The Foundation for Local Democracy which shelters victims of domestic violence has over the past two years helped 9 local victims of sex trafficking.[27]
- In 2005, the BiH Government for the first time provided funding for NGO activities and a public campaign in the area of trafficking in human beings. The government contribution was 15,000 €.[28]

Notes:

1. These organizations include: OHR (The Office of the High Representative); UNMIBH (United Nations Mission in Bosnia and Herzegovina, which was replaced by the EUMP (European Union Police Mission) on 1 January 2003); IPTF (The International Police Task Force); UNHCR (United Nations High Commission for Human Rights); SFOR (Stabilization Force of the Partnership for Peace); OSCE (Organization for Security and Cooperation in Europe);

and numerous NGOs.

2. From a report prepared by OHCHR and UNMIBH.

3. *Reuters*, 11 November 2000.

4. *Associated Press*, 30 July 2001.

5. *UN Wire*, 5 March 2001.

6. *Agence France Presse*, 15 November 2001.

7. *[Stop-traffic] News/ Balkans*, 18 October 2002.

8. *Agence France Presse*, 8 June 2002.

9. *Reuters*, 1 August 2002.

10. *International Herald Tribune*, 21 October 2002.

11. *[Stop-traffic] News/Bosnia*, 13 February 2003.

12. *Transitions Online (TOL)*, "The Ultimatum from Washington," 26 June 2003. See <http://www.tol.cz/>.

13. *BBC News*, 2 August 2001.

14. *Washington Post*, 29 May 2001.15. See:<www.humanrightswatch.org/reports/2002/bosnia/>.

16. *Oslobodjenje*, 29 November 2004.

17. Operation "Macro" was based on cooperation between the Ministries of the Interior and UNMIBH.

18. *Victims of Trafficking and Violence Protection Act of 2000: Trafficking in Persons Report*, (Washington, D.C., U.S. Department of State 2005).

19. Ibid.

20. Bar, nightclub and brothel owners often do not charge police for the sexual services that they receive from trafficked women under their control.

21. Articles have been written about the involvement of police in trafficking in the magazine Panorama, published in Bijeljina, and in the weekly magazine *Dani*, published in Sarajevo.

22. *Dnevni Avaz*, 18 September 2003.

23. Nezavisne novine (Independent news), June 7,2005.

24. *Bosnia Daily*, July 26, 2005.

25. *Victims of Trafficking and Violence Protection Act of 2000: Trafficking in Persons Report*, 2005.

26. *Bosnia Daily,* July 26, 2005.

27. Ibid.

28. Ibid.

Chapter 14

Bulgaria

COUNTRY OF ORIGIN
COUNTRY OF TRANSIT
COUNTRY OF DESTINATION

*Ten minutes and I can get you a girl – any girl
– blond, brown, black or white," declared Mitko,
working late at night in the streets around Sofia's
most luxurious hotels, taking pride in his ability
to quickly deliver what his customer want. The
girls in his books are all aged between 16 and
20."Maximum 20" was what he declared.*

*A pimp in Bulgaria's capital city of Sofia
BBC NEWS, 12 May 2005
http://news.bbc.co.uk/1/hi/business/4532617.stm*

OVERVIEW

Bulgaria's transition from a centralized to free market economy
has been difficult, as with all the countries in Southeast Europe,
but its economy began to stabilize in 1997 and due to this
stability, Bulgarian citizens no longer need visas to visit the
countries of Western Europe. Even so, the transition to a market
economy and privatization have greatly reduced the number
of jobs in the labor market. And, like elsewhere in Southeast
Europe, women were the first to lose their jobs and were harder
hit by the economic difficulties.

Bulgarian women have been more vocal and organized
about the problem of trafficking than women in other countries of
Southeast Europe. They have cooperated with law enforcement
in both Bulgaria and abroad, taken part in investigations, and
testified against traffickers. Because of their efforts, the number
of Bulgarian women trafficked abroad is decreasing.

BULGARIA AS A COUNTRY OF ORIGIN

Bulgarian women are trafficked to many countries: Greece,
Macedonia, Kosovo, Turkey, Italy, and Cyprus. They are also

trafficked, less frequently, to the Czech Republic, Poland, Germany, the Netherlands, Spain, Austria, and France. Bulgarian women who are trafficked come predominately from the border areas of the northeast, in particular from the cities Ruse, Dobrc, and Varna, all of which are on or close to borders. A disproportionately high number of women and girls trafficked out of Bulgaria belong to the Roma minority.

BULGARIA AS COUNTRY OF TRANSIT

Trafficked women and girls who pass through Bulgaria on their way to Western Europe come from Moldova, Romania, Ukraine and other countries of the former Soviet Union.

BULGARIA AS COUNTRY OF DESTINATION

In recent years, due to its economic stabilization and rise in quality of living standards, Bulgaria has also become a destination country. During the summer season, women from elsewhere in Southeast and Eastern Europe work in the Bulgarian sex industry. It is not clear how many of these women are trafficked and working in conditions of forced prostitution.

SOME PROSTITUTION AND TRAFFICKING STATISTICS

Although the dominant opinion in Bulgarian society is that trafficked women in general come from ethnic minorities or are generally uneducated and very young village girls, research by the Bulgarian NGO Animus/La Strada, shows that this is not the case. The composition of sex-industry workers in Bulgaria is as follows:

- 47% are ethnic Bulgarians
- 35% are ethnic Roma from Bulgaria
- 18% are from Romania, Ukraine, Russia, Moldova, and other countries.

The age breakdown of victims of trafficking is as follows: 50% are between 16 and 20 years old, 20% are between 21 and 30, and the remainder are over 30. Out of 43 recent Bulgarian victims of trafficking 7% were from Sofia, 55% were from other cities, and 38% were from villages. Of the 26 women from the group who were interviewed, all had at least a high school education, but some of them had interrupted their studies due to economic difficulties, trafficking, or other reasons.[1]

In the year 2000, 679 Bulgarian women were deported from other countries and returned to Bulgaria. The majority were deported from Germany, Poland, and Greece.[2] It is not clear how many of those deported were victims of trafficking. One estimate claims that 1,200 out of the 10,000 Bulgarian women involved in prostitution are in Poland.[3] And yet according to the Bulgarian Ministry of Interior, just 100 Bulgarian women are working as prostitutes in France, only 2,000 in the EU, and only 3,000 in Bulgaria and abroad.

Between March 2000 and August 2001, IOM (Sofia) assisted 63 trafficked women and girls. Of these victims, 35 were of Bulgarian origin and had been trafficked to Kosovo, Macedonia, Albania, Italy, and Spain. Twenty-five had been trafficked into Bulgaria from Russia, Ukraine, Moldova, Georgia, and Romania.[4] During a 2000 police raid on a bar in Pristina, 26 young girls were rescued and some of them were from Bulgaria.[5] In 2000, a 15-year old Bulgarian girl claimed on German television that she had been sold to a nightclub in Tetovo (a city located in the northwest part of Macedonia, not far from Kosovo). The customers of this night-bar were apparently KFOR[6] soldiers from Kosovo. After this story was broadcast, approximately 100 women and girls were rescued from 16 bars in the towns Tetovo and Gostivar.[7]

In 2001 in Stockholm, three men and one woman from the former Yugoslavia were accused of trafficking 13 women from Bulgaria, Czech Republic, and Slovakia into Sweden, Norway, Denmark and Belgium.[8] Bulgarian women are also trafficked to the Middle East; it is believed that Bulgarian women make up 70% of the foreign women working as prostitutes in Dubai.[9]

Since 1997, the towns of Strasbourg, Mulhouse and Colmar in France have been the final destination for women trafficked from East and Southeast Europe, and in Colmar and Strasbourg the dominant group was Bulgarian. In 2001, young Bulgarian women were seen working as prostitutes in the railway station, but by June 2002, they had been moved to less obvious sites. These young women are believed to be under the control of traffickers living in Germany.[10] In the town of Mulhouse, many of the women in prison arc from Southeast Europe, and Bulgaria in particular. These women were accused of working as procurers. Their trafficking bosses are still at large.[11]

In Loire, France, a Bulgarian network of traffickers was first confronted by police in January 2001, and completely eliminated by December 2002. The group was composed of ten people: eight from Bulgaria, one from France and one from Turkey. Two women from Southeast Europe worked as the bridge between pimps and prostitutes.[12] In November 2003, a story about Bulgarian prostitutes in the city of Nice was broadcast on television.

On August 22, 2002, UNMIK stopped a car carrying an Albanian man and a Bulgarian woman without documents. While the woman was charged with prostitution, UNMIK didn't speak with the Albanian man, even though it appeared that he was a trafficker.[13] According to an IOM report from 2003, women from Kosovo, Bulgaria and Albania sell for less on the market than women from Ukraine and Moldova.[14]

Criminal gangs in Romania and Bulgaria are extremely dynamic and involved in a wide range of criminal activities that significantly impact many European Union Countries, according to a recent Europol report.[15] Bulgarian authorities estimate that international sex trade operatives traffic approximately 10,000 people a year from Bulgaria to other countries. They also smuggle heroin from Asia to West Europe using the same pathways.[16]

According to police in Sofia, approximately 770 Bulgarian pimps are working both at home and abroad.[17] But according to Mr. Boyko Borisov, Interior Ministry Chief Secretary, Bulgarian criminals are no worse than those from Italy or the U.S.

> *Imagine you are a poor, unemployed single mother living in Bulgaria. A woman befriends you and offers to help you and your 11-year-old daughter go to America where a great job is waiting for you. Though you don't speak English or know anyone there, you are so anxious to have a better life that you accept this woman's offer. But when you get to America, your "friend" holds you and your daughter in slave-like conditions and forces both of you to sleep with men for money that she takes as payment for your travel expenses. You are not allowed to leave the house and cannot communicate to seek help. (This story came to the attention of World Relief, which has established the Southeastern U.S. Network of Emergency Trafficking Service.)*

> *Katia, a Bulgarian woman in her late twenties, was recruited by a trafficker to travel voluntarily to France, where she was told she could make a lot of money as a prostitute. Upon her arrival in France, she was met at the airport by the trafficker, who then took away her passport and locked her in a hotel room in a suburb of Paris. She was told that she would have to pay off a travel debt of over 10,000 € by having sex with a minimum of 200 people without being paid. She was kept as a virtual prisoner in the hotel sharing this miserable fate with several other women from Bulgaria, who all worked day and*

night with limited food and water. Finally, Katia
and her colleagues were liberated in police raids.
The police arrested the owner of the hotel, but the
kingpin was in Germany and escaped justice.

TRAFFICKING METHODS AND ROUTES

The main trafficking routes involving Bulgaria are as follows:
*   Eastern countries > Bulgaria > Serbia, Macedonia > Kosovo, Albania > Western Europe
*   Eastern countries > Bulgaria > Macedonia> Greece
*   Eastern countries > Bulgaria > Turkey

In particular, trafficking can be found in the border areas in the southwest of Bulgaria, such as Petrich, which is close to Greece, and Blagoevgrad and Kjustendil, which are close to Macedonia. Organized crime groups that are involved in the trafficking of women and girls arc also involved in drug trafficking, vehicle and human smuggling, and voluntary prostitution. The new Western European visa rules for Bulgarian citizens are creating increasingly sophisticated means of trafficking Bulgarian women.

ACTIONS AND LAWS AGAINST TRAFFICKING

Actions

*   In 2004, the government initiated 399 investigations against police officers which resulted in indictments against two officers for human trafficking charges, three officers for rape, and one officer for forced prostitution. [18]
*   In 2003, the Ministry of Interior identified 104 trafficking victims, and referred 86 of them to IOM.[19]
*   From the beginning of 2000 to the end of 2002, there were 17 police operations against traffickers and smugglers.

Police identified 10 organized criminal groups, and initiated 14 different legal proceedings.

- The Ministry of Health has been active in providing information in HIV and AIDS prevention.
- The Ministry of Education, with assistance from IOM, has introduced informational campaigns for high schools and the general public.
- In 2001, the Ministry of the Interior established a Task Force to Combat Trafficking in Persons for Sexual Exploitation.
- Iv Loiret, France, a Bulgarian network of traffickers was broken up by police in January 2001, and completely eliminated by December 2002. The group was composed of 10 people: 8 from Bulgaria, 1 from France, and 1 from Turkey. Two women were the bridge between the pimps and the prostitutes, who were from Southeast Europe.[20]

Laws And Prosecution

The Bulgarian government has been focused on anti-trafficking legal reform and law enforcement since 1999 when fighting trafficking was defined as a priority issue. In 2001, the Bulgarian government, with assistance from the local NGO Animus/La Strada, began drafting comprehensive legislation to address the issue of human trafficking. The law was aimed at protecting and supporting victims of trafficking.

In August 2002, the Bulgarian government approved the first reading of a bill combating human trafficking that provided for the formation of a "National Anti-Human Trafficking Committee." The bill is based on international conventions used in the fight against trafficking calling for witness protection and the formation of local committees similar to the national committee.[21] The following year, the Bulgarian Parliament moved this bill into a law on Combating Illegal Trafficking in Human Beings. This new law can serve as an example for the region as it combines the issues of prevention, victim assistance, and principles of human rights. The law criminalizes all forms of trafficking in persons and fulfills international obligations. Potential prison sentences range from 5 to 15 years and property may be confiscated. New legislation also provides witness protection including coverage for victims of trafficking and also special protection measures for victims and their families who are cooperating with investigations and prosecutions of traffickers. The government also created a special provision allowing for residency and employment of trafficking victims while they participate in criminal proceedings. [22]

Bulgaria has actively implemented this new anti-trafficking legislation, and reported seven convictions and 27 indictments for suspected trafficking cases under the new trafficking provisions of the criminal code. The government also reported 900 sentences for trafficking-related offenses, including forced prostitution, inducement to prostitution, and people smuggling. In addition, the National Investigation Service developed a methodology for investigating trafficking cases, which it distributed to police. [23]

PROBLEMS

According to a Bulgarian police source, two local towns, Sandaski and Petrich, have become regional sex trade centers – marketplaces for women and girls from East and Southeast Europe. Greek police sources say, the subsequent transfer of women from Bulgaria to Greece is well organized and controlled by criminals. Apparently a trafficker in Sandaski, who is well-known to officials, controls the entire enterprise, even including the taxi firms that are used by traffickers. This man is apparently either protected by or simply tolerated by local law enforcement.[24]

In the last several years, Bulgarian organized crime has slowly but surely made inroads into Western Europe, particularly in Germany and France. Bulgarian criminals in Western Europe cooperate with criminal organizations in Bulgaria, with the unfortunate end result of increased profits from human trafficking including the sale of infants.[25]

WORK BY NGOS AND INTERNATIONAL ORGANIZATIONS

IOM and the NGO Animus/La Strada provide assistance to trafficked women – both to Bulgarian women who have been trafficked abroad, and to women who have been trafficked into Bulgaria.[26] Both IOM and La Strada programs provide safe transportation, departure and arrival arrangements, documents, escorts in transit, financial support, and a reintegration program. IOM had been using the shelters of local NGOs, but in 2002 moved into its own shelter, which can provide long-term accommodation and reintegration assistance for trafficked women. Unfortunately, at this time, while both IOM and La Strada cooperate with police, they do not cooperate with each other. Financial support for fighting trafficking and supporting victims of trafficking in Bulgaria comes from international organizations and donors such as US AID, IOM, UNDP, and the US Department of Justice.

There are varying claims of success for reintegration programs. One source claims that 80% of the women who are trafficked and then returned to Bulgaria once again return to prostitution abroad.[27] However, IOM claims that its victim reintegration has been more successful, and that of the 35 Bulgarian women they have assisted, only four have returned to work in the sex industry. IOM also cooperates with the Bulgarian Red Cross, which has six shelters for vulnerable and homeless children.

La Strada has done important work with its informational campaign. It has organized round tables, collected data, made proposals for the National Plan of Action against trafficking, and used the press and a lobbying campaign to inform the public about the issue of trafficking and to help people understand that human trafficking is a violation of human rights. Another group, Nadia Centre, offers psycho-social services for female victims of various forms of violence.

Finally, it should be noted that although there are Bulgarian programs for HIV/AIDS prevention, these programs are aimed at sex workers of Bulgarian origin - not at sex workers from other countries.

Notes:

1.This information comes from the Bulgarian-based NGO "Animus"/La Strada.
2. This information comes from the National Coordinator of the Stability Pact Task Force.
3. *Reuters*, 16 November 2001.
4. Limanowska, *Trafficking in Human Beings in Southeastern Europe*, (Belgrade: UNICEF, UNOHCHR, OSCE/ODIHR 2002) 53.
5. *CTK National News Wire*, 20 September 2000.
6. KFOR is an international military force responsible for establishing a security presence in Kosovo.
7. *Stop-Traffic News*, 23 December 2000.
8. *Scottish Daily Record and Sunday Mail*, 1 February 2001.
9. *CTK National News Wire*, 19 September 2000.
10. *Prostitution et société* - hors serie, decembre 2002.
11. Ibid.
12. *Prostitution et société*, octobre-decembre 2002.
13. See Amnesty International's report entitled: "So Does It Mean That We Have the Rights?" published in 2004. The report condemns the role of international
peacekeepers in Kosovo (UNMIK).
14. Ibid.
15. *Sofia News Agency*, 15 October 2004.
16. Ibid.
17. *MSNBC* 2003.
18. *Victims of Trafficking and Violence Protection Act of 2000: Trafficking in Persons Report*, (Washington, D.C., U.S. Department of State, 2004).
19. *Victims of Trafficking and Violence Protection Act of 2000: Trafficking in Persons Report*, (Washington, D.C., U.S. Department of State, 2003).

20. *Prostitution et Societe*, octobre-decembre 2002.

21. *Radio Free Europe/Radio Liberty* online report 16 August 2002. See: <http://www.iwpr.net>

22. *Victims of Trafficking and Violence Protection Act of 2000: Trafficking in Persons Report,* 2004.

23. *Victims of Trafficking and Violence Protection Act of 2000: Trafficking in Persons Report*, (Washington, D.C., U.S. Department of State, 2005).

24. *Balkan Crisis Report*, Institute for War and Peace (IWPR), No. 460, 15 September 2003.

25. BBC News, 21 February 2005.

26. La Strada also runs the Centre for the Rehabilitation of Women, Adolescents, and Children Victims of Violence.

27. This estimate comes from the Bulgarian-based NGO "Animus"/La Strada.

Chapter 15

Croatia

COUNTRY OF TRANSIT
COUNTRY OF DESTINATION

OVERVIEW

Although the 1991-1995 war in Croatia undermined economic development and social stability, Croatia's transition has been proceeding faster and smoother than most other countries in Southeast Europe. Compared to Bosnia and Herzegovina, the presence of international organizations and military forces was brief, small, and not overly disruptive, and by 2000, Croatia had normalized international relations. The unemployment rate has remained lower than elsewhere (about 10%) and cases of domestic violence have not increased here the way they have elsewhere. Because of these and other factors, Croatia is not in general considered to be a country of origin for human trafficking.

Very little information has been collected on trafficking in Croatia. There is also a lack of agreement on how serious the problem of trafficking is. Local NGOs regard trafficking as a marginal problem, but international organizations warn that the problem is serious and mostly hidden. The U.S. State Department, in its Annual Trafficking in Persons Report for 2004, put Croatia on its "Watch List for Tier 2," noting the government's inability to identify victims and follow through with appropriate law enforcement action and to provide enough support for activities to combat trafficking. In 2005, Croatia was Tier 2, but no longer on the "Watch List."

CROATIA AS A COUNTRY OF TRANSIT AND DESTINATION

The information available on trafficking in human beings for the purpose of sexual exploitation, suggests that Croatia is a country of transit. There are reports, however, that the country is increasingly becoming a destination country especially during the summer months when women are trafficked from Bosnia and Herzegovina to the resort towns on the coast. According to statistical data available, the percentage of trafficked women and children is very small in comparison with other countries of the region.

SOME PROSTITUTION AND TRAFFICKING STATISTICS

*   In 1999, six Croatian men in France were sentenced to 4-6 years in prison for procuring women from Eastern Europe for the purpose of prostitution.[1]

*   Between 1998 and 2000, 24 cases of human trafficking were found in Croatia. The majority of women involved came from Hungary, Ukraine, and Romania, and included two girls under the age of 18.[2]

*   According to a 2001 report by the Ministry of Labor and Social Welfare of Croatia, approximately 12 trafficked women from Croatia were found in Spain, Switzerland and Italy.[3]

*   In 2002, 7 foreign women in Croatia were identified as victims of trafficking; 5 were from Moldova and 2 were from Ukraine.

*   In September 2003, one citizen of Croatia and two citizens from Bosnia and Herzegovina were arrested by police while smuggling two Albanian men from Macedonia over the Croatian border en route to Italy[4]. These people were long time smugglers and traffickers.

ACTIONS AND LAWS AGAINST TRAFFICKING

Actions

In 2001, the Ministry of the Interior was chosen to coordinate anti-trafficking activities in Croatia. In May 2002 the Croatian government established a National Committee for Suppression of Trafficking in Persons. In 2004, the government adopted a national plan of action, appointed an anti-trafficking coordinator, and provided direct funding to implement the plan. The government has improved cooperation with NGOs, and in partnership with IOM has implemented an anti-trafficking training program expected ultimately to reach 1,600 police officers.[5]

Laws and Prosecution

In 2004, 4 people were sentenced for trafficking in human beings with sentences of 7 months to 9 years.[6] In October 2004, the Government of Croatia enacted a new law prohibiting and punishing offenses relating to trafficking in persons. The new legislation provides for penalties from 1 to 10 years' imprisonment and when the victim is a minor, the minimum sentence is 5 years. Penalties are the same as those for rape.[7]

Also in 2004, the Croatian Parliament amended its Law on Foreigners to increase the length of time that trafficking victims can apply for temporary residency status, from 90 days to 1 year, with a possible 1 year extension.[8]

PROBLEMS

Corruption remains a problem throughout Croatia. Government efforts to identify victims, provide protection, and create greater awareness about trafficking in human beings are still weak although the government has funded new anti-trafficking awareness campaigns.[9]

WORK BY NGOS AND INTERNATIONAL ORGANIZATIONS

• In November 2000, OSCE organized a Round Table on Trafficking that was attended by representatives of the Parliament, Ministries of Foreign Affairs, Justice, Interior, NGOs, and

Stability Pact Task Forces on Trafficking.

• In 2002, IOM gave assistance to women from Moldova and supported the work of local NGO, "STOP," in the assistance of two women from Ukraine.

• In 2004, the government and NGOs co-funded several prevention programs, a shelter, a hotline, a public awareness campaign, and law enforcement training for law enforcement. The Ministry of Education, in partnership with IOM, trained 272 teachers on how to present trafficking to students.[10]

• IOM and NGOs participate on mobile anti-trafficking teams that assist in identifying victims and providing assistance.

• The Center for Women War Victims (ROSA) is active, and has the support of IOM and ICMC.

• ICMC provides training for PETRA , the NGO network in Croatia.

Notes:

1. *Czech News Agency*, 6 January 1999.
2. Alexander Stulhofer, et al. *Trafficking in Women and Children for Sexual Exploitation,* (Zagreb: IOM, 2002) 18.
3. Report presented on Conference in Stubicke Toplice in May 2001.
4. *Dnevni Avaz*, September 13, 2003.
5. *Victims of Trafficking and Violence Protection Act of 2000: Trafficking in Persons Report*, (Washington, D.C., U.S. Department of State, 2005).
6. Ibid.
7. Ibid.
8. Ibid.
9. Ibid.
10. Ibid.

Chapter 16

Republic of Macedonia

COUNTRY OF TRANSIT
COUNTRY OF DESTINATION

OVERVIEW

The Republic of Macedonia, like other countries in the region, has become a transit and destination country for traffickers moving women from Eastern and Southeastern Europe into Western Europe. The problem has escalated in the last few years, especially since the Kosovo crisis, when the level of organized crime dramatically increased. The increased international presence has also had a strong influence on prostitution and trafficking, particularly in the western part of Macedonia.

The March 2001 conflict with the Albanian National Liberation Army (UCK) in the western part of Macedonia isolated this region of the country, and allowed organized crime and human trafficking to flourish. However, this brief period is over, and the government has made significant efforts to comply with the minimum standards for eliminating human trafficking. Even so, in its Trafficking in Persons Report for 2005, the U.S.State Department dropped Macedonia from Tier 1 to Tier 2, because in 2004, the government did not make sufficient progress in strengthening its anti-trafficking efforts. Although the country passed new anti-trafficking legislation in 2004, it failed to demonstrate significant improvement in enforcement and prevention.

MACEDONIA AS A COUNTRY OF TRANSIT

Macedonia is a transit country for trafficking in women and girls for forced prostitution in the region of Struga and Ohrid in the south, and towns of Tetovo and Gostivar, where the population of the western part of the region is predominantly Albanian.

Women and girls from Eastern Europe and elsewhere in Southeast Europe are trafficked via Macedonia to Albania, Kosovo, or Italy. They enter Macedonia legally or illegally from Serbia and Bulgaria. The illegal channels for exiting the country are from Dojran and Gevgelija to Greece and from the region of

Struga to Albania.

MACEDONIA AS A COUNTRY OF DESTINATION

Women and girls trafficked into Macedonia come primarily from
Ukraine, Moldova and Romania. The introduction of a Shengen
visa for Bulgarian citizens means that the number of Bulgarian
women trafficked into Macedonia has decreased.

SOME PROSTITUTION AND TRAFFICKING STATISTICS

The number of trafficked women in Macedonia is very difficult
to estimate. According to one police report, there are between
2,400-2,600 trafficked women in Macedonia at any given time.[1]
Another report, based on information from local NGOs, estimates
the number to be somewhere between 1,500 and 2,500.[2] Accurate
figures are another problem. According to a variety of sources,
including local NGOs, trafficking in Macedonia is not growing.
The actual number of victims of trafficking is, however, unknown,
and there is no data on the number of internally trafficked women
and children for the purpose of sexual exploitation.

The International Organization for Migration (IOM),
which has its own center in Skopje, assisted 213 trafficked
women and girls in 2002 and 95 during the first half of 2003.
Half of those assisted were from Moldova, 30% from Romania,
11% from Ukraine, and the rest from Bulgaria, Russia, and
elsewhere.[3] Between August 2000 and November 2001, IOM
Skopje helped 328 trafficked women return to their countries
of origin: 60% to the Republic of Moldova, 27% to Romania,
and the rest to Ukraine, Belarus, Bulgaria, Russia and Kosovo.
Twelve percent of these victims of trafficking were under the
age of 18.[4]

In September 2001, police organized raids in Vilesta, a
village located in the southwestern corner of the country, close
to the border with Albania and well known as a place with many

bars that serve KFOR soldiers on weekend leave from Kosovo. Fifteen women from Moldova and Romania were rescued during the raid and placed in a shelter.[5]

A reminder of just how profitable human trafficking is: Ali Ahmety, the leader of a Macedonian rebel group, conceded in an interview with MSNBC.com that some of the rebels' funding might come from narcotics trafficking and the flourishing sex slave trade in the region. But Ahmety maintained that the volume of donations to the rebel movement made it impossible to check their source.[6]

Many stories have been collected from women and girls who were victims of trafficking in Macedonia:

> *One woman from Lviv, Ukraine worked in Greece for three years, but on her train trip home to Ukraine, she was kidnapped by two men in Bulgaria, who subsequently trafficked her to Macedonia. After two weeks she tried to escape with a client who offered to help her, but her escape attempt was unsuccessful: the client was severely beaten, and she was returned to a sex bar where she was held for eight months.[7]*

> *Another Ukrainian woman, who was told in Odessa that there was work for her abroad, was trafficked to Yugoslavia (now Serbia and Montenegro), and then forced by her Serbian traffickers to enter Macedonia by foot. Once in Macedonia, she was brought to Kumanovo and then sold to a bar owner from Velesta where she was forced to work without pay – she finally managed to escape to the Ukrainian embassy.[8]*

> *"Natasha" was sold by her friend in Moldova, and was then trafficked through Romania, Serbia*

*and Kosovo to Macedonia. In Velesta, she was
bought by Meti, an ethnic Albanian pimp, and
forced to have sex with more then 1000 men
during her nine months in the village, working in
the bars "Bela Dona" and "Club 69". Natasha
was finally rescued by a client and brought to the
IOM shelter in Skopje.[9]*

*"Olga" was also kidnapped in Moldova and
then trafficked through Romania and Serbia to
Macedonia, where she was also bought by Meti
and forced to engage in sex work in Velesta,
where she was finally rescued by Macedonian
police. Often victims of trafficking who end up in
Macedonia are trafficked into Albania or Greece
after a few months, because customers become
"tired of them.[10]*

*"Luisa," a 32-year-old Moldovan single
mother, thought she was getting a job in Italy,
but instead found herself in Velesta working as
a sex slave for Bojku Dilaver Leku, an ethnic
Albanian trafficking kingpin who is considered
a "most wanted person" both by local police
and European law enforcement officials. She
was freed in a police raid on Velesta after
MSNBC.com confronted Macedonia's interior
minister with stories about sex slavery in the
village.[11]*

Many of the victims of trafficking in Macedonia are minors. In
December 2000, a 16-year-old Bulgarian girl was sold in a night
bar in Tetovo and forced to have sex with clients.[12] In Skopje,
in April 2001 three girls aged 16, 17, and 18, who had been
trafficked in from Romania and Moldova escaped from the bar

where they had been forced into prostitution and found their way to the IOM shelter in Skopje.[13]

TRAFFICKING METHODS AND ROUTES

- East Europe > Romania > (Serbia, including Kosovo)> Macedonia > Greece, Albania > Italy
- East Europe > Romania > Bulgaria > Macedonia > Greece, Albania > Italy
- East Europe > Romania > Bulgaria > Macedonia > Kosovo > Montenegro, Albania > Italy

ACTIONS AND LAWS AGAINST TRAFFICKING

Actions

- In 2004, the Government of Macedonia assisted 38 victims at its Transit Shelter Center, a significant decrease from the 143 victims it assisted the previous year when the Ministry of the Interior set up a shelter for victims of trafficking with the capacity to assist 20-30 people.[14]

- In June 2001, the Macedonian government signed an agreement with IOM that obligated police to inform IOM about women and girls who are irregular migrants. The police should first identify women or girls who may have been trafficked and then transfer them to a shelter in Skopje where IOM makes a second assessment.

- The Ministry of Foreign Affairs mandated that consular officers receive training on victim identification. Consular officers may not independently issue visas for women in the so-called entertainment industry and must send all requests through an Internal Affairs review board.[15]

Laws and Prosecution

In 2002, Macedonia adopted amendments to the country's
criminal law and criminalized trafficking and actions that
are associated with trafficking. In 2004, the Government of
Macedonia amended its trafficking law to establish mandatory
minimum sentences of eight years' imprisonment for traffickers
in cases where there are aggravating circumstances. Under
Macedonian law, victims may be granted refugee status or
asylum. The country has no witness protection law, but recent
amendments to the criminal code contained some witness
protection provisions. and the government seeks to ensure
protection for all victims. The police have provided 24-hour
protection for victims testifying in court.[16]

In 2002 there were several prosecutions, including
the notorious "Kumanov" case, in which the traffickers were
accused and convicted of smuggling and other offences related
to prostitution. Moldovan and Romanian women were brought
back to Macedonia by the Ministry of Interior in cooperation
with NGOs and IOM to testify against their traffickers.

In 2004, the government investigated 39 cases of human
trafficking cases, charged 38 persons, and submitted 19 cases
for prosecution. Four defendants were sentenced to 12 years in
prison. [17]

PROBLEMS

If Romania is often the beginning of a trafficking journey and
Albania the end (before victims of trafficking go to Italy and
other countries in Western Europe), Macedonia plays the role
of a key midpoint because of its poorly patrolled borders, which
are ideal for traffickers.[18]

A serious problem in Macedonia is judicial and law
enforcement ineffectiveness. An example of this is the case of
Dilaver Bojku Leku who escaped June 30, 2003 from the Struga

prison, where he was serving a six-month sentence for forcing a woman into prostitution. Leku controls the biggest prostitution ring in Macedonia, running 10 bars in the region, and recruiting Moldovan, Romanian and Ukrainian women and girls who have been victims of trafficking. He had been arrested in Struga on February 7, and sentenced to just six months in prison, apparently due to lack of evidence.[19] Leku escaped to Montenegro, where he was eventually caught and extradited on July 4, 2003. The case of Leku's escape attracted the attention of the international community, which was eager to see a crackdown on organized crime in this region. Apparently, the case so irritated the US Ambassador to Macedonia that he asked officials: "Are you afraid, are you corrupt, or are you just incompetent?"[20]

In 2004, he was back in prison serving a sentence of 3 years and 8 months for "mediation in prostitution," but was in an "open regime," which allowed him to regularly leave the prison on his own recognizance. In March 2005, he was retried for additional charges, but the court failed to safeguard the victim-witness's identity or prevent the defendant from intimidating her and court officials. [21]

WORK BY NGOS AND INTERNATIONAL ORGANIZATIONS

Unfortunately, for a long period of time the local NGOs were not interested in taking on anti-trafficking activities, and only the Association of Macedonian Women (AMW) has been active in this field since 1999. Now the new organization La Strada Macedonia, which is cooperating with La Strada Bulgaria, is also working on anti-trafficking activities.

Local NGOs working on anti-trafficking activities include: Open Gate, Caritas, and HOPS. There are also several organizations engaged in anti-trafficking activities in Macedonia, including IOM, UNICEF, UNHCR, and OSCE.

Notes:

1. *New York Times*, 28 July 2001.
2. Limanowska, *Trafficking In Human Beings in South Eastern Europe*, (Belgrade: UNICEF, UNOHCHR, OSCE/ODIHR, 2002) 53.
3. IOM press briefing notes, 23 March 2001 and 6 April 2001.
4. Limanowska, 109.
5. Limanowska, 108.
6. For the full story, see:<http://www.msnbc.com/news/667790. asp?0sp=v3a8>.
7. *Trafficking in Women: Moldova and Ukraine*, (Minneapolis: Minnesota Advocates for Human Rights, 2000) 27.
8. *New York Times*, 28 July 2001.
9. For the full story, see: <http://www.msnbc.com/news/744312. asp?0sp=v3a5>.
10. For the full story, see: <http://www.msnbc.com/news/725802. asp?0sp=v3a2>.
11. Ibid.
12. *Agence France Presse*, 17 December 2000.
13. IOM press briefing notes, 6 April 2001.
14. *Victims of Trafficking and Violence Protection Act of 2000: Trafficking in Persons Report*, (Washington, D.C., U.S. Department of State, 2005).
15. Ibid.
16. Ibid.
17. Ibid.
18. *Balkan Crisis Report*, Institute for War and Peace (IWPR), No. 460, 15 September 2003. See: <http://www.iwpr.net>.
19. *Balkan Crisis Report,* No. 440, 30 June 2003.
20. *Balkan Crisis Report,* No. 460, 15 September 2003.
21. *Victims of Trafficking and Violence Protection Act of 2000: Trafficking in Persons Report,* 2005.

Chapter 17

Romania

Soho is the heart of London's sex trade and is mostly under the control of foreigners. Last year 15 year old "Natasha" gave evidence against a pimp who had forced her to have sex with customers for 20 hours a day. She had come from Romania over the Balkans to London. Also a 16-year-old girl from Romania gave evidence against two Albanians who trafficked and raped her. She had been sold at 12 and trafficked via Macedonia to London.

The Guardian, March 26, 2003

In his documentary, "Cutting Edge: The Child Sex Trade," Romanian filmmaker Liviu Tipurita filmed a boy living in a cardboard box in Bucharest. He and his friends survive from the little money they earn mainly from begging and selling sex. His clients are from Britain, Holland, Switzerland and Germany. From Bucharest, Tipurita travelled to Milan, where the film showed how Romanian boys, some as young as 10, were being pimped for underage sex, often by their own fathers, brothers, and cousins.

Wsws. org., October 25, 2003

OVERVIEW

The transition to a market economy has been particularly hard for Romania, whose population is suffering from drastically reduced income levels and lack of access to social services. The number of jobs available has been severely reduced, and women were the first to be affected by rising unemployment. At present, unemployed young women have very little chance of finding a job in the labor market, and even if they do find work, chances are good that the income from one job will be insufficient to support them or their families. The feminization of poverty in Romania has caused mass migration of women to cities and abroad. It has also increased the number of women working in the sex industry in Romania. Both of these factors have increased opportunities for traffickers to take advantage of Romanian women and girls.

The United States State Department currently identifies Romania as a "Tier 2" country, that is, a country that does not meet the minimum standards for fighting trafficking in human beings. However, as a result of this classification, the Romanian Government has identified the fight against trafficking as a priority, and as an integral part of the war on organized crime.The Romanian Government hosts the headquarters for the Southeast European Cooperative Initiative (SECI). In 2004, Romania actively participated in SECI anti-trafficking operations including "Mirage 2004."[1]

ROMANIA AS A COUNTRY OF ORIGIN

The majority of trafficked Romanian women come from the northwest part of the country, known as Romanian Moldova – the major towns involved are Iasi and Suceava. There are also reports that Romanian teenage boys are working in the sex industry in Western European countries.

ROMANIA AS A COUNTRY OF TRANSIT

Romania is a center for trafficking. Women and girls are brought into Romania from Moldova, Ukraine, and other countries of the former Soviet Union. From Romania they are trafficked out into Serbia, Bosnia and Herzegovina, Albania, Turkey, Italy, and Greece. In 2003, the routes of trafficking changed, partially as a result of the January 2002 policy allowing Romanian citizens to travel without visas to European Union countries. In 2003, less victims were trafficked to former Yugoslav countries and more to Western Europe.[2]

ROMANIA AS A COUNTRY OF DESTINATION

Most of the women working in the sex industry in Romanian cities are Romanian, and many of them belong to Romania's ethnic Roma minority. However, it is estimated that 20% of Romanian sex workers are foreigners – it is not clear how many of these women are victims of trafficking.[3]

SOME PROSTITUTION AND TRAFFICKING STATISTICS

* 20% of sex workers in Romania are women and girls from other countries.
* 30% of sex workers in Romania are under 18 years of age.

Over 200 cases of trafficking in women and girls were reported to the Romanian police in 1999. The Balkan states and Italy were the most common destinations.[4] In November 2000, 33 women were discovered in bars in Prijedor (in the northwest part of Bosnia and Herzegovina). Many of them were from Romania. The women told UN police that they had been forced into prostitution.[5] Between January 2000 and July 2001, 484 trafficked women and girls were returned and repatriated to Romania from abroad – these returns were assisted by IOM and local NGOs. About half of these women were from Romanian Moldova, and half of the repatriated victims were girls under the age of 18. Their trafficking destinations were as follows:

* 30% returned from Bosnia and Herzegovina
* 28% returned from Macedonia
* 18% returned from Albania
* 11% returned from Kosovo
* 6% returned from Italy
* 3% returned from Cambodia
* 4% returned from other countries.

Romanian women and girls make up a disproportionately high number of trafficking victims in the Balkans. In Albania and Bosnia and Herzegovina, there are estimates that 35% of the trafficked women are from Romania. In Kosovo, it has been estimated that 10% of the trafficked women are from Romania, and in Bulgaria, 22% of the trafficked women assisted in 2000 were from Romania.[6] In Bosnia and Herzegovina, 25% of women who working in bars claim to have been forced into prostitution. Most of them come from Moldova, Romania and Ukraine.[7] According to IOM Kosovo, 71 out of the 303 women that they assisted in the period from February 2000 to April 2002 were from Romania.[8]

Romanian women and children (both girls and boys) have been reported in Bosnia and Herzegovina, and in Serbia and Montenegro including Kosovo. Romanian women and children can also be found in Western European countries such as France, Luxembourg, Belgium and the Netherlands. Turkey, Albania, Italy, Spain and Ireland are also destination countries for victims of trafficking from Romania.[9]

The first destinations in Romania for people being trafficked through are Timisoara, Turnu and Severin. From there they are usually trafficked across the border into Serbia.[10]
Romania is not known as a country attractive to sex tourists, but there have been some cases of pedophilia involving foreign men. One case involved a German man who had sex with several children.[11]

Romanian police action in 2002 destroyed 74 networks that were involved in trafficking. In total, 589 people were detained: 462 were prostitutes and 127 were people otherwise involved in trafficking, some of whom were from Western European countries. In 2003, two men and a woman in Cluj, Romania were arrested and charged with forcing hundreds of women from Romania and the former Soviet Union to work as prostitutes in Spain. They were part of a ring, which transported approximately 300 women to Spain between 1997 and 2003.[12] In March 2003 several Romanian trafficking rings were dismantled in Spain when 32 out of 39 people detained were Romanian.[13]

A survey of newspaper stories on trafficking and Romania shows that compared with the number of stories in 2001 and 2002, the number of stories in 2003 was significantly lower. This can be taken as an indication that the Romanian government has been increasingly successful in combating trafficking, and that new visa regulations in Western Europe are also resulting in a decrease in trafficking (although apparently not a decrease in prostitution).

STORIES FROM ROMANIA

One story, which comes from UNICEF, is of a 12-year old Romanian girl who asked a friend to help her escape from her abusive father. Instead of receiving help, she was sold to Serbia, where she was forced to work as a prostitute, and then trafficked into Macedonia, Albania and Italy, where she was resold. She finally ended up as a prostitute in the UK, where she escaped from her owners and ended up in the care of social services.[14]

Another story is of Helena, a 17-year old girl who was brought from Romania to Italy to work cleaning houses, but instead she was forced into prostitution by the man who brought her into the country. He had beaten and raped her, and said that if she did not work as a prostitute on the streets her family would be killed. Helena, along with five other girls, was eventually rescued by the Italian police.[15]

This story comes from Porte Douphie in Paris. "Three Romanian boys are drinking beer on the streets of Paris. Eighteen-year old Gregoire, a handsome boy with blue eyes, has lived in France for almost 5 years. His smile is frozen and deformed. The other two are just 13 and completely drunk. They are Gregoire's cousins and have just arrived in France from Romania. They smoke as if they were adults and stay on this spot all night awaiting customers. On the other side of the street is 25 year old Stephen. He has been in the sex business for 10 years and looks depressed. 'With those young boys from Romania, I haven't got a chance. The clients prefer young 'meat' and in a competition with them, I am the loser.' On another Paris street corner, another young Romania boy, about 11 years old, is also involved in prostitution but is never picked up by the police. Because he is so young, it never even occurs to the officer in charge that he could be selling himself as a prostitute." [16]

"My story is a simple one," says Milena, who managed to escape her captors and return home to Romania where she is now in a shelter run by the NGO - Reaching Out. "I got pregnant and had a child on my own. Shortly after giving birth, a friend took care of the baby and I got a job. I found a place to live but soon started to have financial problems. I couldn't cope, and some friends suggested that I try working abroad. I was thinking it might be a good solution for awhile until I got back on my feet; I never thought that I would end up working as a prostitute".

Milena worked as a prostitute in Austria. Since prostitution is illegal in that country, her captors made sure she spent her days locked in a dark room. She was so depressed that the other girls who worked with her took pity on her and managed to collect 200 € so that she could pay her way back home.[17]

Anna is another young woman living in the shelter. She is only 15 years old. In her room at the shelter there are toys, dolls, and books. Anna left home at age 12 and slept on the stairs of an apartment building. Looking for a job, she stumbled upon a woman who promised her a brighter future. But the woman was actually part of a trafficking network and Anna was soon forced to become a prostitute. At age 14, Anna was given a passport and sent to Turkey, where she was soon caught by the police and sent home. But back in Romania, the same woman was waiting for her and sent her to Spain. There she was forced to go out with clients at night. Finally, a kind man helped her escape back to Romania.[18]

(more stories can be found at www.iwpr.net)

TRAFFICKING METHODS AND ROUTES

Women being trafficked usually travel in small groups. They enter countries with either no documentation or legal documents that include tourist visas for Bulgaria, Albania, and Serbia. From these three countries, they sometimes continue on to other countries.

The main trafficking routes into Romania are:
* Moldova, Ukraine, > Romania

The main trafficking routes out of Romania are:
* Romania > Serbia, Bosnia and Herzegovina > Albania > Italy, Greece
* Romania > Hungary > Western Europe or Serbia

The route from Romania to Serbia is usually via Timisoara.

ACTIONS AND LAWS AGAINST TRAFFICKING

Actions

In 2001, Romania established a national task force on trafficking and an Inter-Ministerial Committee. This Inter-Ministerial Committee on Trafficking has representatives from the Ministry of Foreign Affairs, the Ministry of the Interior, the Ministry of Justice, the Ministry of Education, and the Ministry of Research.

The committee drafted the Romanian National Plan of Action, with assistance from the South-East Cooperation Initiative and the FBI of the United States. The Ministry of Foreign Affairs is also working with the government of the Republic of Moldova to create an anti-trafficking program that includes the sharing of information and experience on drafting anti-trafficking laws and the creation of an institutional network to combat trafficking. However, this program currently does not include plans to prosecute traffickers, fight corruption, or close down trafficking routes.

As a result of the National Plan of Action:

* Romania has increased the amount of education about human trafficking in the form of informational campaigns, lectures,

seminars, and training led by the Institute for Research and Criminality, which is part of the Ministry of the Interior.

- The issue of human trafficking has been introduced into the school curriculum by the Ministry of Education, with assistance from IOM.
- The Ministry of Health is working on a program of health protection for vulnerable groups.
- Local experts are gathering data and creating reports on human trafficking in Romania.
- Stricter border control as of 2001 has decreased the number of migrants entering Romania without legal documents; this has most likely lessened the amount of trafficking into Romania.

In 2004, the government approved a National Action Plan to prevent and combat trafficking in children, and in June 2004, the police opened the Trafficking Resources Center to centralize the collection of country-wide trafficking data. The government has also spent considerable effort to improve protection for trafficking victims. In 2004, it opened five of nine trafficking shelters required by law, compared with only two opened in 2003. Also, the government provided funding to a local NGO to open ten shelters for unaccompanied repatriated children, and they have already assisted 32 trafficked children. The Ministry of Administration and Interior provided security at Bucharest's non-government-run shelter that assisted 100 victims throughout 2004.[19]

Laws and Prosecution

Romania's anti-trafficking legislation specifically covers trafficking for the purposes of both sexual and non-sexual exploitation and provides for appropriate penalties. In 2004, the country adopted new laws which improves anti-trafficking protection of minors and provides protections for victims of all crimes, including trafficking. According to the new law victims are entitled to shelter, legal, psychological, and social assistance. However, government funding for NGOs that assist trafficking victims remains low.[20]

In 2003, the Romanian authorities convicted 49 traffickers. In 2004 the number of convictions significantly increased to 103 traffickers. Those convicted in 2004 received prison sentences of from one to 10 years.[21]

PROBLEMS

Problems remain in the struggle against trafficking in Romania. Corruption among law enforcement officials remains a serious problem. In 2004, Romania's lead police anti-corruption agency investigated 81 police officials thought to be involved in trafficking-related corruption. Administrative sanctions were imposed on 31 officials, 10 were dismissed, and 40 cases were sent forward for prosecution. Also, in 2004, the Anti-Corruption National Prosecutor's Office also reviewed a total of ten cases in which trafficking related corruption was suspected.[22]

The judicial system is still weak, and not able to deal with the problem effectively. In addition, the system sometimes targets the victim in the legal process and not the perpetrator – for example, victims who have testified against traffickers have later been arrested for prostitution and illegal border crossing based on their testimony. The Romanian police, who are always included in the process of returning women who have been trafficked back to Romania, also sometimes accuse trafficked women of having been illegal migrants or voluntary prostitutes.

At the end of 2002, 400 Romanian women were deported from Spain and flown by charter to Romania. Despite evidence that these women were trafficking victims and had asked the Spanish police for help, the Romanian police upon their arrival in Romania treated them all as if they had been deported from Spain as illegal migrants.

The second major problem is with victim assistance. Romania still doesn't provide foreign women who have been trafficked into Romania with interpreters or information in their native language. There are no programs providing victims with alternative means of settlement instead of returning them to their home countries – victims do not have the right to apply for asylum or to claim welfare. The basis of this problem is financial: there simply isn't the money to provide these services.

There is also a problem of internal trafficking reflected in the expanding prostitution industry within Romania, especially in Bucharest. At the moment there is little interest in this issue except from some journalists. According to reports, the prostitutes who are victims of this internal trafficking work under the poorest conditions in which pimps sell them to other pimps and move them from place to place.[23] Police report there is evidence of growing involvement of the Roma community in this form of human trafficking.

Finally, while the trafficking of children is becoming a serious problem in the country, it is not recognized by the authorities. For years, EU countries have had information about young unaccompanied children from Romania who beg and pickpocket on the streets or, in the worst cases, are victims of sexual exploitation. Currently there is no specific program with a focus on trafficked children. Girls under 18 returning under the IOM program are treated as adults. However, there are plans to offer specialized support to child victims in the near future.

WORK BY NGOS AND INTERNATIONAL ORGANIZATIONS

For many years, NGOs were the only organizations directly involved in the assistance and reintegration of trafficked women and children in Romania. The first NGO to provide this assistance was "Reaching Out," based in Pitesti. Most NGO-run shelters and organizations are based outside of Bucharest.

IOM is very active in victim assistance, and has built a

shelter that offers assistance to trafficking victims 24 hours a day. They also offer repatriated women tests for HIV and for sexually transmitted diseases. IOM has started to build a new network of NGOs, incorporating NGOs that don't have previous experience assisting victims of human trafficking. Some NGOs, however have chosen to remain independent such as Reaching Out Shelter in Pitesti.

These NGOs have organized into a new network called FAMNET, and have expressed some concern about IOM's approach to sending women back home to the same environment from which they were trafficked – without help finding a job or reintegrating into society. FAMNET has established a telephone hotline and informational materials for women.

Notes:

1. *Victims of Trafficking and Violence Protection Act of 2000: Trafficking in Persons Report*, (Washington, D.C., U.S. Department of State, 2005).
2. *Victims of Trafficking and Violence Protection Act of 2000: Trafficking in Persons Report*, (Washington, D.C., U.S. Department of State, 2004).
3. Ibid.
4. *Irish Times*, 12 March 2001.
5. *Associated Press*, 15 November 2000.
6. This statistic comes from Bulgaria's National Service for Combating Organised Crime, located in the Ministry of the Interior.
7. *Associated Press*, 30 July 2001.
8. IOM Kosovo, Situation Report – Feb. 2000 to April 2002.
9. *A Human Rights Report on Trafficking of Persons, Especially Women and Children*, The Protection Project, Washington, D.C. March 2002.
10. *Newsday*, 13 March 2001. See also IOM Press Briefing Notes, 6 March 2001.
11. *Agence Frace Presse,* 10 January 2001.
12. *Associated Press*, 29 January 2003.
13. *Lavanguardia*, 29 March 2003.
14. *BBC News*, see:< http://news.bbc.co.uk/go/pr/fr/-/2/hi/uk_news/3107461.stm>.
15. Ibid, see:< http://news.bbc.co.uk/go/pr/fr/-/2/hi/europe/3103460.stm>.
16. *Le Nouvel Observateur*, 20-26 Decembre 2001: 94-98.

17. See <http://www.unicef.org/sowc05/english/povertyfeat_romania.html>.

18. Ibid.

19. *Victims of Trafficking and Violence Protection Act of 2000: Trafficking in Persons Report,* 2005.

20. Ibid.

21. Ibid.

22. Ibid.

23. See <http://www.iwpr.net/index>.

Chapter 18

Slovenia

181

OVERVIEW

When Slovenia became independent from Yugoslavia in June 1991, it was the most developed republic within the former SFRY. The brevity of the war in Slovenia – which lasted only 15 days – and the new country's ability to maintain positive economic trends, meant that its social and economic relations were not undermined by the transition to post-Yugoslavian independence. In May 2004 Slovenia joined the EU. A per capita GDP of \$19,600 and unemployment rate of just 6.4% have ensured a comfortable and stable life for most of the population. Due to these factors, Slovenia is generally considered not to be a country of origin for victims of trafficking, but there are cases in which Slovenia is mentioned as a country of destination or transit for victims of trafficking.

SLOVENIA AS A COUNTRY OF ORIGIN

Comparatively few Slovenian women are trafficked to Western Europe – Slovenia is not considered to be a country of origin.

SLOVENIA AS A COUNTRY OF TRANSIT

Women and girls who pass through Slovenia en route to Western Europe are trafficked from East, Southeast, and Central Europe.

SLOVENIA AS A COUNTRY OF DESTINATION

Slovenia is not considered to be a country of destination. Women who have been trafficked to Slovenia entered the country on work visas as nightclub dancers.

SOME PROSTITUTION AND TRAFFICKING STATISTICS

Between 1993 and 1996, only one case of trafficking was reported to the police, and in 1999, the police reported 20 cases.

The Inter-Departmental Working Group for Combating Trafficking in Human Beings reported that in 2002 police made 55-trafficking-related arrests and prosecutors initiated 21 prosecutions, involving 28 victims, 15 whom were considered victims of enslavement.[1]

TRAFFICKING METHODS AND ROUTES

Slovenia borders Croatia, Hungary, Austria and Italy. The Slovenian borders with Austria and Italy run along the Alps and are full of forests, valleys, and caves, which form terrain ideal for the trafficking of irregular migrants into Austria and Italy by organised crime. In 2000 alone, the number of border violators was 35,892.

ACTIONS AND LAWS AGAINST TRAFFICKING

Actions

The Ministry of the Interior is engaged in an informational campaign to raise awareness among potential victims of trafficking, and has printed up pamphlets and other materials. There is a National Coordinator for Trafficking in Persons and in 2004, the government adopted a National Action Plan to Combat Trafficking in Human Beings, but has had difficulty implementing it because of budgetary pressures.[2]

Laws

In March 2004, Slovenia amended its penal code to criminalize trafficking. Traffickers are also prosecuted for related criminal offenses including pimping, procurement of sexual acts, inducement into prostitution, rape, sexual assault, bringing a person into slavery or a similar condition, and the transportation of slaves.

PROBLEMS

Traffickers are rarely prosecuted in Slovenia partially because it is difficult to get convictions. One reason for this is an absence of a witness protection program which Slovenia is now considering how to establish and implement. In 2004, the U.S. Department of State put Slovenia on its "Watch List" for Tier II because of its "modest efforts" to prosecute traffickers in 2003.[3]

On December 9, 2004 the *Solvenia Bulletin* reported how Slovenia had been affected by the death of Olena in Bosnia and Herzegovina.

> *Last month's death of a Ukrainian prostitute in Bosnia has apparently struck fear into not only her former clients but among johns (customers) throughout Slovenia. The girl, Olena Popik, was a victim of human trafficking who worked as a prostitute in Slovenia for two years, as well as in Croatia, Serbia and Bosnia and Herzegovina. At the time of her death, she had TB, syphilis, hepatitis C and AIDS. The clinic in Slovenia noted a spike in requests for STD testing when the news of her death broke, and now the daily "Finance" is claiming that some Slovenia night clubs are registering a 90 percent drop in business because their strippers are from Ukraine.[4]*

WORK BY NGOS AND INTERNATIONAL ORGANIZATIONS

The government supports a local NGO which has established a 24 hour hotline for trafficking victims and does education outreach in the schools. In late 2003, the government made an agreement with a local NGO that runs Slovenia's shelter to provide victims with protection from prosecution, temporary residence status, and social services.[5]

Notes:

1. *Victims of Trafficking and Violence Protection Act of 2000: Trafficking in Persons Report*, (Washington, D.C., U.S. Department of State, 2003).
2. *Victims of Trafficking and Violence Protection Act of 2000: Trafficking in Persons Report*, (Washington, D.C., U.S. Department of State, 2004).
3. Ibid.
4. Slovenia Bulletin, December 9, 2004. See: <http://slo-bulletin.blogspot.com/2004_12_05_slo-bulletin_archive.html>.
5. *Victims of Trafficking and Violence Protection Act of 2000: Trafficking in Persons Report*, 2004.

Chapter 19

The State Union of Serbia and Montenegro including Kosovo

COUNTRY OF ORIGIN
COUNTRY OF TRANSIT
COUNTRY OF DESTINATION

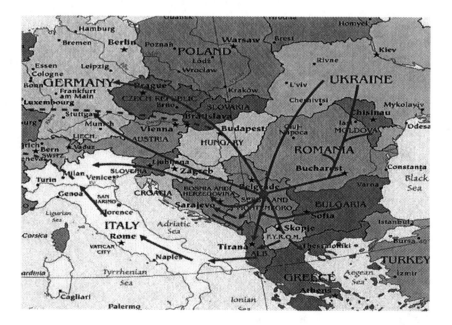

Human trafficking in the State Union is still viewed as an isolated social and criminal phenomenon approached separately from other social and economic problems.

Mary Black, UNICEF Program Chief in Serbia and Montenegro, Beta New Agency, May 5, 2005

OVERVIEW

The State Union of Serbia and Montenegro is composed of the Republic of Serbia and the Republic of Montenegro. Following the 1999 NATO intervention and UN Security Council Resolution 1277, the UN administers the province of Kosovo within the Republic of Serbia. In this chapter we will examine human trafficking separately for each of the three regions in this State Union, because it has developed differently in each location.

After the dissolution of the former Socialist Federal Republic of Yugoslavia (Slovenia, Croatia, Bosnia and Herzegovina, Serbia and Montenegro including Kosovo, and Macedonia) and the beginning of the war in the region, the international community imposed sanctions on and isolated the Federal Republic of Yugoslavia. The economy was destabilized, causing poverty and hardship throughout the country.

Organized crime developed alongside the sanctions and was linked to and incorporated into the police system of the State. Since 1991, organized crime has undertaken step-by-step the trafficking of cigarettes, alcohol, stolen cars, drugs, weapons, and women and girls for the purpose of using them in the sex industry. The organized crime groups from Serbia and Montenegro cooperate closely with gangs in East and Southeast Europe.

Although political changes on October 5, 2000 resulted in the lifting of economic sanctions, the State Union of Serbia and Montenegro is still a poor country where organized crime is well-established. However, after the March 2003 assassination of Prime Minister Zoran Djindjic, the government organized strong measures against organized crime under the title "Sablja," and this action has resulted in the elimination of several criminal groups and gangs. Unfortunately, however, the situation in Serbia remains almost the same as it was at the beginning of 2003.

SERBIA AND MONTENEGRO AS A COUNTRY OF ORIGIN

Serbia and Montenegro is a country of origin. There are various recruiting methods in the country, including advertisements for business escorts and waitresses and personal advertisements for marriage offers, lonely hearts, etc. According to data from 1997, 32 such agencies were registered in Belgrade alone.

SERBIA AND MONTENEGRO AS A COUNTRY OF TRANSIT

Serbia and Montenegro is primarily a country of transit, and Belgrade is the crossroads for trafficking women and girls to Bosnia and Herzegovina, the southwest part of Serbia (specifically, the region of Sandjak), Kosovo, Montenegro, and Macedonia.

SERBIA AND MONTENEGRO AS A COUNTRY OF DESTINATION

Organized crime groups in Serbia often traffic women in from Eastern Europe and Romania and bring them to Belgrade, where they are distributed to two southern regions in Serbia: Sanjak and Kosovo. Major destination cities include Kraljevo, Krusevac, and Nis.

Serbia

SOME PROSTITUTION AND TRAFFICKING STATISTICS

There is no reliable data on the trafficking of women and girls from Central Eastern Europe to Serbia. According to the police, a total of 1,260 women from East European countries tried to enter the then Federal Republic of Yugoslavia (FRY) illegally in 2000 and were stopped at the border. However, the police did not register the entries of young women from Moldova, Romania, and Ukraine who came to FRY in tourist groups and with legal documents, but actually were entering the state to work in the sex industry. This type of entry is organized by travel agencies operating in the countries of origin.[1]

Between January 2001 and June 2003, 138 women and girls were identified and assisted as victims of trafficking: 124 were foreign, and the remaining 14 were domestic.[2] The majority of the victims, approximately 45%, were from Moldova; 30% were from Romania, 15% were from Ukraine, and 10% were from Serbia. According to Vesna Stanojevic, the Belgrade shelter for victims of trafficking had assisted 58 women by January 2003. Six additional women were expected to arrive at the shelter at the time of the report, including a Moldovan woman who was in the hospital after escaping from her captors by jumping from the third floor of a Belgrade building.[3]

Traffickers from Serbia have strong links with pimps in Romania. They jointly organize the trafficking of women and girls via Romania to Serbia, usually without difficulty.[4] Serbian prostitution rings also buy women from Eastern European traffickers and then sell them to Albanian traffickers, who smuggle many of the women into Kosovo.[5] In July 2001, three Serbian men were arrested in Moldova for their involvement in trafficking in human beings for the purpose of sexual exploitation. They were charged with recruiting and trafficking women from Moldova to Belgrade.[6]

Trafficking routes run from Ukraine, Hungary and Romania through Belgrade into Kosovo; there is also trafficking between Serbia and Montenegro, and trafficking to Albania and Italy.[7] Women trafficked in from Eastern Europe often pass through a specific house in Belgrade, where they are sold at auctions. Women judged to be particularly good looking are often sent to Bosnia and Herzegovina to stay for a period of time, after which they will be sent on to Greece or Italy. Those women considered less attractive are sent immediately to Kosovo or Albania.[8] On December 5, 2002, the Belgrade daily paper *Novosti* reported that Serbia had become one of the main transit centers for trafficking in persons for the purpose of sexual exploitation.[9]

ASTRA, a women's NGO in Belgrade, launched an awareness campaign called "Open Your Eyes," designed to inform young women and girls about advertisements for good jobs which are in fact potential trafficking traps.[10] Unofficial data suggests that 60 young women and girls in Serbia are missing persons.[11]

One potential victim of trafficking from Belgrade responded to an advertisement in a daily newspaper, and after submitting the requested documents, was informed that she had been granted a job in a Western European country and was invited to a meeting at the agency. Her mother accompanied her to the meeting with the "agent," and insisted on seeing the contract, job description, salary, and working conditions. The agent refused to give her the requested information, and finally told the mother, quite angrily, that the daughter did not have to accept the job offer. The mother immediately filed a report with the police, but by the time they arrived at the agency, both the agent and the agency had disappeared from

*that address. At least two other women did fall
prey to this advertisement: one woman ended up
in Japan as a sex slave, but was able to return
to Belgrade due to fortunate circumstances. The
second woman was not as lucky: she called from
the United Arab Emirates after several years,
asking for help – but after that telephone call, all
traces of her were lost.*

The daily paper *Blic*, claims that Belgrade is the largest sex trafficking center in the region. Blic also noted that in the past, live auctions have been organized at the "Arizona" market. ("Arizona" is a black market in the northeast part of Bosnia and Herzegovina, close to the border with Serbia).[12]   One young woman, "Elena," left Romania and illegally crossed the Yugoslav border in order to reach Italy and visit her family. However, the smuggler she hired, instead of helping her, brought her first to Belgrade and then to a nightclub in "Arizona," where she was forced into prostitution.[13]

In 2001, Serbian police arrested Miroslav Stankovic, a Serb in the village of Trgoviste near Bujanovac, on suspicion of trafficking 146 women into Kosovo. Based on this arrest, police were able to uncover a smuggling chain trafficking Romanian, Moldovan and Ukrainian women from Belgrade, Stara Pazova, Pancevo and Nis.[14]

The assasination of Prime Minister Zoran Djindic in March 2003, increased government action against organized crime. One result of subsequent police actions against prostitution was to move the problem out of central Belgrade: due to control and raids by the police, the number of bars decreased and much of the business moved from the center to the periphery. Criminals running prostitution rings also changed their methods, increasingly using mobile telephones and keeping trafficking victims in private apartments.[15]

The paid-sex scene has changed as well in Novi Pazar,

the capital city of Sandzak (a region in Serbia). Once Novi Pazar was a strip-bar centre, where wealthy local men were encouraged to spend 2-3,000 euros per night on shows, drinks and sex. However, the city instituted an anti-organized crime policy, which forced owners of strip bars to pay taxes that are 25-30 times higher than those for restaurants or cafeterias, and this policy has "killed the business." However, Novi Pazar remains a regional center for trafficking in women and girls who come in from Belgrade, and there are middlemen that direct customers to one of the 25 hidden brothels with foreign prostitutes. Prostitution in Novi Pazar is mostly under the control of one man who lives in Italy, along with approximately ten locals. After a stint in Novi Pazar, many trafficked women travel to Italy via Roane. Interestingly, the local police maintain that they have no information on these prostitution and trafficking rings, although it is said that even little children in the city know the names of the people involved.[16]

According to the Ministry of Interior, in 2002 423 foreign women were identified during police checks as being employed as dancers, hostesses, waitresses, and strip-girls. Of these women, 245 were from Romania, 84 from Moldova, 67 from Ukraine, 10 from Bulgaria, and 9 from Russia. After a detailed investigation, 60 of the women were identified as trafficking victims; of these 32 were from Romania, 13 from Moldova, 9 from Ukraine, 4 from Bulgaria, and 4 from Russia.

According to the NGO ASTRA, between 2002 and 2004, 103 human trafficking victims were registered in Serbia of which 68 were Serbian, and the rest were foreign citizens. In 2004 they had 40 underage registered victims.[17]

The most recent UNICEF report *Trafficking in Human Beings in Southeast Europe (2005)*, as reported in *Danas*, states that the number of victims of trafficking in Serbia in the last 2 years decreased. But NGO ASTRA believes this is only a temporary situation related to the sudden arrests and reorganization of trafficking businesses rather than its disappearance.[18]

Some NGOs commented that the number of victims has actually increased, and that Serbian police reports are unrealistic because they show only the number of foreign women working in hotels and bars rather than the overall number of victims. The UNICEF report also mentioned that Serbia is a transit country for women and girls from Albania, Moldova, and Romania who pass through on their way to Bosnia and Herzegovina, Kosovo, and Macedonia, while women and girls from Serbia are generally sold in Italy and Greece.[19]

On July 13, 2005, *Internet Svedok* reported that "Operation Mirage" conducted in June 2004 found 59 trafficked persons: 34 victims were foreigners and 25 were from Serbia.

TRAFFICKING METHODS AND ROUTES

Trafficking routes into Serbia include:
- Interstations such as Bucharest, Romania and Budapest, Hungary. Trafficking victims are often held in apartments in these two cities for days or weeks before they are transported to Serbia.

Trafficking routes out of Serbia include:
- Belgrade > Bosnia and Herzegovina, Bulgaria > Turkey
- Belgrade > Kosovo > Albania (then on to Italy and Greece)
- Belgrade > Montenegro, Albania > West Europe
- Serbia > (Kosovo) > Macedonia > Albania > Italy
- Serbia > (Kosovo) > Macedonia > Greece

There are many markets for buying and selling women in Serbia. The main markets are in Belgrade, which is the European center for the sale and purchase of trafficked women. Other markets for trafficked women are found in Subotica, on the Hungarian border; in Novi Sad, south of Subotica; and in Nis, northeast of Kosovo.

ACTIONS AND LAWS AGAINST TRAFFICKING

Actions

• In 2000, police arrested 41 traffickers, and between January and September 2001, they arrested over 50 traffickers. Traffickers were accused of smuggling, trafficking and organizing prostitution, restricting freedom of movement and confiscating documents, including keeping a person in slavery.[20] However, in 2000, only two traffickers were prosecuted, and their sentences were suspended. By 2002, only one person had been charged under Article 155.

• At the end of 2000, the Government appointed a National Coordinator on Trafficking and a Coordinator for the Stability Pact Task Force. OSCE established its Mission in FRY and began at that time to pressure the government to include the issue of trafficking in its agenda.

• In June 2001, the National Coordinator launched the Initial Board for Combating Trafficking in Human Beings. The Initial Board formed four working groups with different aims. However, Serbia does not yet have an updated comprehensive National Plan of Action.

• In July 2001, a Belgrade shelter for victims of trafficking in Serbia was opened.

• In 2002 the city established an anti-trafficking team that operates within the Belgrade City Police.

• In 2004, Serbia established two full-time police anti-trafficking units made up of six officers within the organized crime police and nine officers within the border police. The police units have increased trafficking investigations and victim identification.[21]

Laws and Prosecution

In 2004, there were 24 investigations involving 51 suspects. All 25 defendants were convicted in the five trials that were concluded.[22]

In April 2003, the Serbian Parliament adopted amendments to the Serbian Criminal Code. The new law uses a definition of trafficking that corresponds with the Palermo Trafficking Protocol.

The penalty for trafficking of human beings is 1 to 10 years in prison. When there is more than one victim, when trafficking involves abduction, or when the victim is treated in a particularly cruel or degrading way, the sentence is from 3 to 10 years. If the trafficking involves children, the penalty is from 5 to 10 years, but when a victim is over 14, the court considers the issue of consent. This does not correspond with Article 3 of the Palermo Trafficking Protocol under which consent is irrelevant for children under the age of 18.

In 2004, the Interior Minister established temporary residence permits for trafficking victims. Victims may stay for three months unconditionally and may stay an additional six months to one-year residency if they participate in an investigation or prosecution. But if a victim fears that returning home may endanger his or her life, they may be given one year's residency with no requirement for cooperation.[23]

PROBLEMS

According to a 2003 Country Report for Serbia by Regional Clearing Point (RCP), the number of victims of trafficking in Serbia is approximately ten times higher than the number of 138 victims actually identified and assisted within Serbia. Another problem is that there is no witness protection program in place for victims of trafficking in Serbia, and, therefore, victims are often afraid to testify.

At the moment, the collection of data on trafficking is being conducted by several different organizations. This is a problem for the Serbian government, since all the data should be coordinated and integrated, while it currently is not. However, in 2004, the National Anti-trafficking Coordinator, in order to remedy poor statistics-keeping by the judiciary, instructed regional police secretariats to follow up with local prosecutors on all trafficking cases filed during the year.[24]

WORK BY NGOS AND INTERNATIONAL ORGANIZATIONS

For a long period, the NGO sector in Serbia was without internal or external support – as a result, the established NGOs were weak, with limited resources and influence. Now, however, international NGOs such as Kvinna Till Kvinna and Norwegian People's Aid support local NGOs in Serbia. There are also a number of women's organizations in Serbia addressing the problems of violence against women. The Anti-Sex Trafficking Action Project (ASTRA) is a network of women's NGOs dealing with the issue of trafficking in Serbia. This NGO network is very effective and closely cooperates with Montenegro. Local NGOs also manage a hotline.

IOM and other organizations working in the field of trafficking have accepted the rules established by OSCE in November 2001 in the "Guidelines." These Guidelines describe the system of identification for a victim of trafficking and the support which should be given to her. Identification must be carried out by the representatives of government, international organizations and NGOs, and the goal is to establish a system of victim protection.

Also acting in Serbia and cooperating with the government are the following organizations: ICMC, UNICEF, UNOHCHR, UNDP UMCOR, Council of Europe, CARE, Cooperazione Italiana, and Swiss Agency for Development & Cooperation. IOM and local NGOs from Belgrade provide the majority of assistance for foreign and national victims. Romanian and Ukrainian consular representatives contact IOM in Belgrade directly for assistance in repatriation of their citizens who are most likely victims of trafficking.

Montenegro

SOME PROSTITUTION AND TRAFFICKING STATISTICS

Regional conflict in the former Yugoslavia has promoted criminal networks, and organized crime has been incorporated throughout Montenegro. Montenegro is a destination and transit country for trafficking in human beings. Historically, the Montenegro Government's response to trafficking was very weak, but they have slowly started to support anti-trafficking actions, to give assistance to victims of trafficking, and to cooperate with international organizations and NGOs. However, NGOs and international organizations believe that a considerably higher number of victims of trafficking have not been identified and thus never received assistance.

In the early 1990s, Montenegro was primarily a transit area for the trafficking of women and girls, who passed through on their way to Albania and Western Europe. In the past several years, Montenegro has become a destination for woman from Moldova, Romania, Ukraine and Russia. However, women who end up in Montenegro are sometimes trafficked on into Albania and then on to Italy. Local NGOs recently reported that several women from Montenegro were arrested in Albania.[1] In addition, a tourist agency from Podgorica trafficked women from Romania and Bulgaria to Croatia in cooperation with a tourist agency from Dubrovnik.[2] The sex industry in Montenegro is located in bars, clubs and motels in Podgorica, Berane, Rozaje and on the coast in the areas of Ulcinj, Bar, and Budva.

Information and statistics from the Ministry of the Interior of Montenegro show that a great number of women who enter Montenegro come in with legal documents, usually valid one-month tourist visas. Some of these women have legal contracts with Serbian agencies or with Montenegrin bar owners. When their legal residency permits and visas expire, these women are detained by the Montenegrin authorities and deported back to the border between Montenegro and Serbia, where they are usually picked up by the mafia. Nobody knows just how many women and girls are trafficked into and throughout Montenegro. According to an RCP Country Report, at least 33 Montenegrin and foreign trafficked women and girls were identified and assisted within Montenegro between January 2000 and June 2003. The majority of the victims were from Moldova, followed in number by women from Romania and Serbia. Three of the victims were from Montenegro.[3] Both local NGOs and international organizations believe that the actual number of victims is significantly higher.

One shelter, "Women's Safe House," was established in 1999 as the first shelter for victims of domestic violence in Montenegro. In 2001 they also founded a shelter for victims of sex trafficking, and since then they have provided safe accommodation, medical, legal, and psychological assistance to 56 women, mostly from Southeast Europe and countries of the former Soviet Union.

Montenegro has long been known as a transit point for human trafficking. The victims generally come from Moldova, Romania, and Ukraine. The mostly Russian and Albanian traffickers pass their human "cargo" into the hands of their Montenegrin colleagues. But Montenegro is also a destination country, as was shown by the scandalous arrest of Deputy State Prosecutor Zoran Piperovic on November 30, 2002. He was charged, along with his friend Bajram Orahovac, a restaurant owner, for his involvement in the trafficking of a prostitute.

The scandal began on November 23, 2002, when Irfan Kurpejovic and Ekrem Jesavic were detained on the basis of a police statement made by a Moldovan victim of trafficking.

According to IWPR sources, the Moldovan woman, "SC", was "owned" by Kurpejovic, who then sold her to Jesavic.[4] According to the daily newspaper Vijesti, Piperovic had been involved in "relations" with SC since 1998, when he took her from a pimp in the Bosnian town of Bijeljina, brought her to Montenegro, and then sold her to "Oscar," the owner of a Podgorica nightclub. It is not clear how Kurpejovic and Jesavic then came into possession of this Moldovan woman.[5]

The "Moldova Case" became public in December 2002, and put the government of Montenegro in a very uncomfortable situation with regard to criticism from the EU, OSCE, CoE, Stability Pact, and the US Government.   They criticized Montengro for how they are dealing with trafficking and victims of trafficking. This scandal continues to influence Montenegro's political scene, especially since the May 20, 2003 decision of Zoran Radonjic, the Senior State Court Prosecutor, not to indict any of the suspects charged with human trafficking and facilitating prostitution. He stated that there was not sufficient evidence to start legal proceedings.[6] This decision by Radonjic evoked a strong reaction from local NGOs, and officials from the US, European Union, CoE, OSCE and the Stability Pact. US Ambassador to the OSCE Stephan Minikes told the Permanent Council in Vienna on June 5, 2003 that the US was "deeply disappointed" that the prosecutor had closed the high-profile human trafficking case without indicting any of the suspects. In addition, United States Helsinki Commission Co-Chairman Rep. Christopher H. Smith expressed outrage on June 11, 2003 that criminal charges were dropped against the four men in Montenegro, including a deputy state prosecutor, in a case in which the victim had been raped, tortured and severely beaten for more than three years while enslaved in prostitution.

LAWS AND ACTIONS AGAINST TRAFFICKING

Actions

• The Government of Montenegro appointed a National Coordinator for Trafficking in February 2001. The government is also participating in the development of a victim protection system and is showing willingness to cooperate with NGOs.

• In March 2001, the Inter Agency Working Group on Legal Reform was established. The National Coordinator on trafficking, OSCE, CoE, American Bar Association, Central and Eastern European Law Initiative, Associations of Attorneys and of Lawyers, and Law Faculty of the Podgorica University participate in the Group. The group's major goal has been the preparation of amendments to the existing laws to ensure victim protection, witness protection and the prosecution of traffickers.

• In September 2001, a Special Task Force on Border Control and the Special Task Force on Trafficking and Smuggling were established.

• The Ministry of the Interior of Montenegro established bilateral contact with its neighboring countries: Bosnia and Herzegovina, Albania and Italy on human trafficking issues.

• In December 2002, Montenegro signed the Tirana Statement on Commitments regarding the legalization of the status of victims of trafficking, including temporary residence permits to foreign victims of trafficking. However, Montenegrin legislation does not yet include a legal approach for temporary residence visas for victims of trafficking.

Laws and Prosecution

In July 2002, the Parliament of Montenegro adopted amendments to the Criminal Code stipulating penalties in connection with trafficking in human beings. Penalties range from 1 to 8 years in prison. In the case of a minor (a child under the age of 14), the penalty is from 1 to 10 years in prison. Those involved in the organization of trafficking activities can face up to 5 years in prison. In April 2004, the government adopted a new criminal procedure code that allows for enhanced surveillance techniques and lesser sentences for those suspects who cooperate with an investigation. It also passed a witness protection law which can be applied in cases of human trafficking. A police anti-trafficking team was reestablished in April 2004, and subsequently submitted six cases to the judiciary. The government brought charges against 18 persons suspected of trafficking violations and initiated five prosecutions involving 14 people.[7]

PROBLEMS

While the government is more actively investigating cases of trafficking, Montenegro's judiciary remains weak; judges exhibit little understanding of trafficking cases, allow long delays in trafficking prosecutions, and impose inadequate sentences upon conviction.[8] There are many stories of traffickers and owners of sex slaves who are released by judges, like one Montenegrin nightclub owner who was told that the next time he might be sentenced to one month in prison. The combination of lack of legislation and a lack of desire to prosecute traffickers means that the response to trafficking remains weak.

WORK BY NGOS AND INTERNATIONAL ORGANIZATIONS

Cooperation among the police, NGOs and international organizations is improving and the police and NGOs have signed a Memorandum of Understanding, which deals with the assistance of trafficked women and girls.

In June 2001, an SOS hotline began operations. This hotline receives phone calls from Serbia, Vojvodina and Bosnia and Herzegovina, where families call to get information about their relatives involved in sex industry. The hotline has also received several phone calls from trafficked women. A Podgorica shelter for trafficked women was opened by the NGO Women's Safety House in October 2001. IOM is also assisting trafficked women in the shelter, but only those who qualify for its program of return.

The OSCE has established the Inter Agency Working Group on Trafficking with the participation of the Ministry of the Interior, IOM, UNICEF and two local NGOs (Women's Safe House and Montenegro Women's Lobby), pushing these various organizations to work together. At the end of 2000, the working group developed the Victim's Protection Project (VPP) for 2000-2002. The VPP is based on international human rights standards and the experience of the participants, but there are still some gaps in protection, such as: lack of support for Montenegrin victims of trafficking abroad; lack of attention paid to internal trafficking; problems with witness protection; and problems for those victims who are not identified by the police or prosecutor as victims and might therefore be charged with prostitution or, if they are foreigners, be deported.

Kosovo

OVERVIEW

Kosovo has a unique status in Europe. It is part of the Republic of Serbia, but after the March 1999 conflict and subsequent NATO intervention, it has been governed since June 1999, by a United Nations Interim Administration (UNMIK).[1] A UN Peacekeeping force has responsibility for international security and peacekeeping operations. Elections in November 2001, were followed by the establishment of a new National Assembly and new government in 2002. However, much government administration and infrastructure building is still under UN control – this includes the police (both UN police and civilian police are under the control of the UN Interim Administration) and justice systems.

According to the Kosovo police, the majority of men who patronize Kosovo brothels are local, but clients do include men serving in the international institutions set up by the UN, in particular KFOR soldiers. In addition, some members of UN institutions have been repatriated under suspicion of their involvement in trafficking.

KOSOVO AS A REGION OF ORIGIN

Due to the growth in poverty, unemployment, and violence against women in Kosovo, it has become a region of origin for women who are trafficked abroad.

KOSOVO AS A REGION OF TRANSIT

Kosovo is a transit point for trafficking from Servia into Macedonia and Albania.

KOSOVO AS A REGION OF DESTINATION

Women and girls who are trafficked into Kosovo are from Albania, Bulgaria, Macedonia, Moldova, Romania, and Ukraine.

SOME PROSTITUTION AND TRAFFICKING STATISTICS

According to the Trafficking and Prostitution Investigation Unit (TPIU) in Kosovo, there are currently 1,000 women and girls in 85 brothels in Kosovo, five of which are in Pristina: it is not clear how many of these women and girls are the victims of trafficking.[2] UNMIK police estimate the presence of 104 brothels in Kosovo where women and young girls are forced into prostitution or unpaid labour.[3] Between February and April 2002, IOM in Pristina assisted 303 foreign women and girls: 52% were from Moldova, 23% from Romania, 13% from Ukraine, 5% from Bulgaria, 3% from Kosovo and Albania, and 1% from Russia.[4] In 2000 and 2001, OSCE assisted 254 women and girls who were victims of trafficking.[5]

According to an RCP report for Kosovo between December 2000 and May 2003, 640 foreign and Kosovar trafficked victims were assisted within Kosovo. The number of foreign victims was 354 and the number of Kosovar victims was 286.[6]

Kosovar victims are mostly girls and women of ethnic Albanian origin. According to statistics from NGOs, approximately 50% of the victims are between 15 and 18 years old, 30% are between the ages of 11 and 14, and 20% are between 19 and 31.

Faketa was kidnapped by young Albanian men on her way to school in Pristina three years ago. She was taken to a bar where she was raped by the owner and his friends and then forced to work as a prostitute. She was allowed to return home in the evenings but she was threatened by the kidnappers who told her they would ruin her reputation if she said a word to anyone. For this reason Faketa didn't tell her parents what had happened to her. Finally she could no longer tolerate her situation and she told her parents what was happening to her. The case finished in court where Faketa testified against the men, but they were released for "lack of evidence."

Kosovo Institute for War and Peace,
August 2002

TPIU estimates that 90% of the foreign women and girls working in the sex industry in Kosovo are victims of trafficking. However, only about 50% identify themselves as victims. This is possibly because they are frightened of their pimps and of retribution by organized crime, or because they do not want to return home marked as prostitutes, knowing that this will cause scandals and make them into pariahs. Women in Kosovo brothels who are not identified as victims of trafficking face arrest on charges of prostitution and illegal residence instead of assistance and repatriation.[7] Many women and girls trafficked from Moldova to Kosovo now apparently willingly work as prostitutes. According to a source in UNMIK, they say that sex work is "better than returning to Moldova".[8] An IOM report from April 2002, based on testimony of victims of trafficking, suggests that clients are primarily local men.[9]

Below is the story of a woman who was trafficked through Kosovo.

I was lucky to be arrested during one raid. I was a classic victim of trafficking. I came to Kosovo from Romania. I was sure that I was traveling

*to Italy to become a nurse in a home for retired
people. My trip to Budapest was OK. In Budapest
I had to buy a ticket and fly to Italy. Instead of
going to Italy, the man who was waiting for
me took my passport and brought me by car to
Serbia and then to Kosovo. I was sold and forced
into prostitution. In the beginning I refused to be
prostitute, but he beat me every day and raped
me too. Finally, I had no choice but to become
a prostitute. I was not allowed to go outside the
bar. I was only allowed to see customers. I did
not sleep - only worked, worked, worked. After
the raid, I went back to Romania, but couldn't
find a job. Now, I am in France and working on
the streets of Nice. Before Kosovo I was not a
prostitute. Now I don't care. I only need money,
and that's it."[10]*

TRAFFICKING METHODS AND ROUTES

Among the 200 women and girls assisted by IOM Pristina in
2000 and 2001, 70% were recruited by false job promises and 9%
were abducted. Living and working conditions for the Kosovo
sex industry in general tends to be worse than other places in
Europe. Unprotected sex, lack of medical care, and physical
maltreatment are common.

The main trafficking routes into Kosovo are through
Macedonia and central Serbia. Approximately 5% of victims of
trafficking who end up in Kosovo are reported to have come from
Albania. The main trafficking routes out of Kosovo are through
Montenegro into Albania, or directly into Albania, continuing on
to Western Europe. Women are also trafficked within Kosovo,
including both Kosovo Serbs and Kosovo Albanians; more
Kosovo Albanians are victims of trafficking than Serbs.

ACTIONS AND LAWS AGAINST TRAFFICKING

Actions

Trafficked women are located and identified via:

- Checkpoints for vehicles
- Raids conducted by the Kosovo Police Service, which are organized by the Trafficking and Prostitution Unit (TPIU). TPIU then takes statements from the women and girls, and when there are indications that they are victims of trafficking, they inform the OSCE Regional Trafficking Focal Point. OSCE then makes a decision to either refer the case to IOM for assistance or contact a shelter for admission.

Laws and Prosecution

In January 2001, a new anti-trafficking regulation was passed, the "Regulation on the Prohibition of Trafficking Persons in Kosovo." Under this regulation, human trafficking is defined as a criminal offence that is punishable by 2 to 20 years in prison. This regulation will also probably be used in conjunction with Regulation No. 2001/4 to confiscate the property of traffickers.

In 2004, UNMIK's Trafficking and Prostitution Investigation Unit (TPIU) conducted 2,386 raids and made 77 arrests.[11]

PROBLEMS

Even though police shut down bars and nightclubs that serve as locations where trafficked women work, court orders reverse these bar closures. Sometimes bar closures that are part of the battle against human trafficking are made under the guise of cleaning up other violations such as lack of necessary documents or health code violations.

There are also problems enforcing the new law within the present judicial and social system:

- Judges often do not understand the problem of trafficking.
- There is only a weak effort to apply this new and "complicated" law.
- The influence of organized crime, omnipresent in Kosovo, along with family and clan relations that are given priority, undermines the rule of law.
- Cooperation between UN police and local police is weak – clan and family relations often supersede official laws and their enforcement.
- It is impossible to provide appropriate witness protection – because their lives are in danger, trafficked women who give police testimony are repatriated before the court dates when they could give testimony in person and serve as witnesses.

On 19 September 2002, *MSNBC News* published a story about Kosovo's judicial system, which allows pimps to stay free and to threaten victims who testify against them; the victims in this story were originally from Ukraine.[12]

According to a recent internal British Government briefing, Albanians or Kosovars now control more than two-thirds of the "massage parlors" in London. Another study noted that organized Albanian gangs are linked with the Kosovo Liberation Army (KLA) running prostitution and sex trafficking rackets across Western Europe. Rome, Milan, Frankfurt, Paris, Amsterdam, Athens and Stockholm are also cities where trafficking in human beings is under the control of Albanians or Kosovars.[13]

WORK BY NGOS AND INTERNATIONAL ORGANIZATIONS

IOM, based in Pristina, leads the way in victim assistance, but assists and repatriates only foreign victims of trafficking. There is currently support service for domestic victims of trafficking, although the Center for the Protection of Women and Children offers limited access to their shelter. OSCE has led the development of policy and procedures to combat trafficking, and also provides some victim assistance.

The international NGO, UMCOR, has been managing a shelter since July 2000, and assists trafficked women referred to them by the IOM repatriation program. Between July 2000 and September 2001, they provided assistance to 232 foreign trafficked women. The average stay in their shelter is two weeks.

Local NGOs are not involved with assistance to foreign victims of trafficking. IOM has organized a campaign to raise awareness of trafficking among local NGOs, and members are also taking part in an OCSE training program on victim assistance.

Local NGOs do run a shelter for women who are victims of domestic violence, and when there is no room in other shelters, they will accept girls under 18, victims of international trafficking, and victims of domestic trafficking. The maximum stay in the shelter is three months.

At the moment there are three shelters managed by local women's NGOs for domestic violence cases, but there is neither sufficient capacity nor resources to offer long-term shelter and services.

Finally, there is the Direct Assistance and Shelter Coordination Working Group, which is a collaboration between IOM, OSCE, UMCOR, and TPIU. This working group also gives assistance to trafficked women in Kosovo and provides a forum that allows both the discussion of individual cases and the coordination of activities.

Although the number of victims assisted in Kosovo has declined; it is believed this is a result of increasingly sophisticated criminal networks responding to anti-trafficking enforcement efforts and shifting the commercial sex trade out of public bars and into private homes.[14]

Notes:

Serbia:

1. Barbara Limanowska, *Trafficking In Human Beings in South Eastern Europe,* (Belgrade: UNICEF, UNOHCCR, OSCE/ODIHR, 2002) 78.
2. *First Annual Report on Victims of Trafficking in South Eastern Europe.* The Stability Pact for South Eastern Europe, The Regional Clearing Point (RCP),2003.
3. *Vesti,* 16 January 2003.
4. *Balkan Crisis Report,* Institute for War and Peace (IWPR), No. 230, 28 March 2001.
5. *Press Review,* AIMpress.org, 24 July 2001.
6. Ibid.
7. Ibid.
8. *Balkan Crisis Report,* 18 April 2002.
9. *Novosti,* 5 December 2002.
10. See: < http://www.iwpr.net/index.pl?archive/bcr2/bcr2_ specialinvestigation_bosniatrafficking_1>.
11. *Nedeljni Telegraf,* 11 December 2002.
12. See <http://www.iwpr.net/index.pl?archive/bcr3/bcr3_2002012_hr_2_ eng.txt>.
13. *Balkan Crisis Report,* 18 April 2002.
14. *Balkan Crisis Report,* 3 December 2001.
15. *Balkan Crisis Report,* No. 460, 15 September 2003.
16. *Vesti,* 10 December 2002.
17. *Portal-NEWS,* 14 January 2005
18. *Danas,* 2-3. April 2005. See <www.danas.co.u/20050402/hronika1. hotmail>.
19. Ibid.
20. Limanowska 80.
21. *Victims of Trafficking and Violence Protection Act of 2000: Trafficking in Persons Report,* (Washington, D.C., U.S. Department of State, 2005).
22. Ibid.
23. Ibid.
24. Ibid.

Montenegro:

1. *Vesti,*15 January 2003.
2. *Vesti,*13 January 2003.
3. *First Annual Report on Victims of Trafficking in South Eastern Europe,* The Stability Pact for South Eastern Europe, Regional Clearing Point (RCP) 2003.

4. *Regards from Montenegro*, Stop-traffic, 11 September 2003. See:<http://www.woman-safety-house.org>.
5. Ibid.
6. *Balkan Crisis Report*, Institute for War and Peace (IWPR), No 448, 30 July 2003. For the full story, see: <http://www.iwpr.net>.
7. *Victims of Trafficking and Violence Protection Act of 2000: Trafficking in Persons Report*, (Washington, D.C., U.S. Department of State, 2005).
8. Ibid.

Kosovo:
1. This interim government was given authority by Chapter Seven of Resolution 1244 of the United Nations Security Council.
2. Limanowska, *Trafficking In Human Beings in South Eastern Europe*, (Belgrade: UNICEF, UNOHCHR, OSCE/ODIHR, 2002) 96.
3. *Return & Reintegration. Project Situation Report*, IOM Kosovo, February 2000 to April 2002.
4. Ibid.
5. Limanowska 98.
6. *First Annual Report on Victims of Trafficking in South Eastern Europe*, The Stability Pact for South Eastern Europe, The Regional Clearing Point RCP), 2003: 75-78.
7. Limanowska 97.
8. *Balkan Crisis Report*, Institute for War and Peace (IWPR), No. 460, September 15, 2003.
9. *Return &Reintegration. Project Situation Report*, IOM Kosovo, February 2000 to April 2002.
10. Interview, Nice 2002.
11. *Victims of Trafficking and Violence Protection Act of 2000: Trafficking in Persons Report*, (Washington, D.C., U.S. Department of State, 2005).
12. See: <http://www.msnbc.com/news/797093.asp?cp1=1>.
13. *Daily Insight*, January 10, 2005. For more data about the heroin and sex trade, see the full story by Jamie Dettmer: http://www.insighmag.com/main.cfm?include=detail&storyid=161254.
14. *Victims of Trafficking and Violence Protection Act of 2000: Trafficking in Persons Report*, 2005.

Chapter 20

Ukraine and
Moldova

Countries of origin

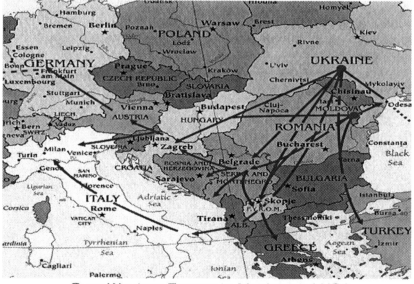

- - - - - - Over Western Europe to Mexico and USA
.... From Odesa to the Middle East

OVERVIEW

Ukraine and Moldova are grouped together in this chapter because their profiles are so similar. These two countries have been especially hard hit by the transition from communism, with social and economic problems including very high unemployment, very low incomes, a significantly lower standard of living, severe social disruption, and slippage in the standards of education, with education costs now out of reach for many.[1]

Ukraine and Moldova now have more people living in poverty, more domestic violence, more prostitution in general, and more women and girls ensnared into human trafficking and forced prostitution.

In Moldova, over half of the population lives below the poverty line. Due to the privatization of land and subsequent corruption, particularly the rural population and agricultural workers have suffered, and this has led to mass migration into towns and cities and abroad. Under the cover of this voluntary migration, women and girls are more easily tricked into becoming victims of trafficking.

Women in particular have been negatively affected by these difficult times, both at home and in the job market. At home, there has been an increase in the amount of domestic violence. In the job market, women lose jobs before men – the unemployment rate for women is more than twice as high as for men. The Human Rights Watch report of August 2003 on discrimination against women in the Ukrainian labor force revealed that the negative policies towards female job seekers continue.[2] The women who do have jobs are paid about 70-80% of what men are paid for similar jobs. Finally, employers are more likely to bring physical and sexual requirements into job descriptions, and to hire only young, attractive women.

There is a steady flow of emigration from both Ukraine and Moldova on a daily basis. Moldovan and Ukrainian citizens working abroad and sending money back home are a significant source of income and support. For example, there are 200,000 Moldovans that take seasonal jobs in Moscow,[3] 200,000 Moldovans working in Italy, 50,000 to 100,000 Moldovans working in Portugal, and between 600,000 and 1,000,000 Moldovans currently living abroad.[4] Along with Romania, Ukraine and Moldova are the largest suppliers of trafficked women in Southeast Europe.

In 2005, the U.S. Department of State placed Ukraine on the Tier 2 "Watch List" because it has not increased its efforts to fight trafficking or made sufficient commitment to do so, particularly in victim protection and prosecution of trafficking-related complicity. However, it is expected that Ukraine's new government, which assumed power in late 2004, will be more effective in finding remedies for institutional weakness and corruption, which hindered anti-trafficking efforts of the previous government.[5]

UKRAINE AND MOLDOVA AS COUNTRIES OF ORIGIN

Ukrainian and Moldovan women and girls trafficked out of the region end up as prostitutes primarily in Albania, Bosnia and Herzegovina, Italy, Kosovo, Macedonia, Greece, Russia, Serbia and Montenegro, Turkey, and increasingly the Middle East - including the UAE and Israel. Women from these two countries are also found in Belgium, the Czech Republic, France, Germany, Ireland, and the UK. The main countries of transit for Moldovan and Ukrainian women are Romania, Hungary, Bulgaria, and Serbia.

SOME PROSTITUTION AND TRAFFICKING STATISTICS

In 1999, the international NGO, La Strada ,estimated that 420,000 Ukrainian women had left the country looking for work abroad; it is not clear how many of these women and girls fell victim to trafficking.

In 2000, Ukrainian police estimated that 20 women were leaving the city of Luhansk each week, and that each month between 500 and 1,000 women and girls emigrate from Donetsk to work abroad. Many of these women and girls end up working in Greece and Turkey as prostitutes.

According to the Ukraine Consular Service, during 1999 and 2000 the Embassies of Ukraine documented several cases of trafficking for the purpose of sexual exploitation of Ukrainian women. In Turkey there were 3 such reports in 1999 and 16 in 2000; in Greece, 3 in 1999 and 2 in 2000; in Croatia, 16 in 1999 and 26 in 2000. The Consular Service also stated that in 1998 there were 6,000 Ukrainian women trafficked to Turkey, 3,000 to Greece, and 1,000 to Serbia.

In Albania in 2000, the dominant group among victims of trafficking who received assistance were from Moldova. In addition, the dominant group among victims of trafficking who passed through Bulgaria in 2000 and 2001 were from Ukraine.

In 2002, IPTF in Bosnia and Herzegovina assisted 199 victims of trafficking: 48% of the victims were from Moldova and 16% were from Ukraine.

According to IOM Belgrade, 48% of the 124 foreign victims of trafficking assisted between 2001 and June 2003 were from Moldova and 16% were from Ukraine. In Montenegro, 33% of the foreign victims of trafficking assisted by IOM between 2000 to June 2003 were from Moldova. IOM in Kosovo assisted 303 victims of trafficking between 2000 and April 2002: 159 of these victims were from Moldova and 38 were from Ukraine.[6] In 2000, IOM in Macedonia assisted 106 victims, 69 of whom were from Moldova.[7] In general, approximately 50% of the victims that have been trafficked within Macedonia were from Moldova, 31% were from Romania, and 11% were from Ukraine. Approximately 10% of the Ukrainian and Moldovan victims of trafficking were under the age of 18.

According to RCP 1,131 Moldovan women and girls were identified and assisted as victims of trafficking between January

2000 and April 2003. This number is based on information provided by the IOM Mission in Chisinau, Salvati Copiii, and La Strada Moldova.[8]

STORIES FROM UKRAINE

A Ukrainian woman, whom we shall call "S.T.," was 29 when she came in contact with an employment office which offered her a job in Belgium. The office paid for her air ticket to Amsterdam where she was picked up by a man and woman who brought her to a bar in Brussels. She was employed in the bar, but, unfortunately, not as a waiter, but as a prostitute and received no money for her work. Eventually, she escaped from the bar and went to a center where she received assistance including legal help to file charges against her traffickers. She was then repatriated voluntarily. The center which assisted the girl in returning home, however, was never informed on the proceedings of the court related to her case.

M.A., a 27 year old woman was smuggled from Ukraine to Belgium by a close relative in order to find a "good job." She took her daughter with her. The relative accompanied her to the immigration office in order to seek asylum - according to the laws of Belgium-, and gave her the necessary documents and then left her alone with her daughter. She subsequently fell into bad company. This man finally took all of her papers, social allowances, and forced her into prostitution. He also trained her daughter to be a prostitute. For over a year she was forced to receive clients during the day when her daughter was in school. Finally she went to the police and declared a case of forced prostitution. The investigation showed that her boyfriend-pimp was also wanted for similar offences in Germany.

Research from Ukraine shows that 65% of cases of trafficking of women from Ukraine were carried out by organized crime groups that possess databases of potential victims gathered from sources such as applications from women who enter beauty contests and marriage agencies.

TRAFFICKING METHODS AND ROUTES

Some young women are coerced by their parents into emigrating to look for better work so they can support their families; the families understand that the young women may end up as prostitutes abroad, but do not understand that they may end up victims of trafficking in conditions of sexual slavery. Also, women who emigrated and ended up as victims of trafficking sometimes return to Moldova and Ukraine and recruit new victims for traffickers based in Western Europe.

The main trafficking routes out of Moldova are:
* Southern part of Moldova (Cahul and Vulcanest) > Timisoara > Serbia > Bosnia and Herzegovina, Kosovo, Montenegro, Macedonia > Albania.
* Southern part of Moldova > Romania > Hungary > Serbia, Romania > Bulgaria > Macedonia > Albania

The main trafficking routes out of Ukraine are:
* Ukraine > Moldova >Romania > Bulgaria > Macedonia > Kosovo or Albania
* Ukraine > Romania, Hungary > Serbia > Bosnia and Herzegovina, Kosovo, Montenegro, Macedonia > Albania

*One Ukrainian woman who was trafficked to
Italy reported that she was taken to the Serbian
border where she was sold to Serbians, and then
taken to Montenegro and sold to Albanians who
took her to Italy.*

*"Eventually I arrived in a bar in Kosovo, and
was locked inside and forced into prostitution.
In the bar I was never paid, I could not go out
by myself, the owner became more and more
violent as the weeks went by; he was beating me
and raping me and the other girls. We were his
'property,' he said. By buying us, he had bought
the right to beat us, rape us, starve us, force
us to have sex with clients." - a 21 year old
Moldovan woman.*[9]

ACTIONS AND LAWS AGAINST TRAFFICKING

Actions

Moldova

- In May 2000, the Moldovan Parliament passed a resolution to create an anti-trafficking working group. This group was supposed to report quarterly on preventative measures, analyze domestic violence, and work on improving the situation of women in Moldova. However, the working group achieved very little, and dissolved with the government changeover in 2001.
- In November 2001, Moldova created the National Committee for Combating Trafficking, and adopted a National Plan of Action for Combating Trafficking.

- According to the 2003 UNICEF report by Barbara Limanovsksa, in 2002 there were 42 trials for trafficking. In just two cases were traffickers sentenced, one to 15 years and the other to 10 years in prison. In 2002 prosecution was also initiated in 49 cases, 30 of which are still pending.
- In January 2005, the government set up a working group with NGO participation to draft a new National Action Plan that will replace the outdated 2001 Action Plan.[10]
- In 2005, local committees working under the National Committee conducted anti-trafficking meetings in schools for teachers and students. [11]

Ukraine

- Ukraine has created a National Coordination Council for Prevention of Trafficking in Human Beings. This council reports to the ombudswoman of the Ukrainian Parliament.
- The Cabinet of Ministers has begun promoting the Program for the Prevention of Trafficking in Women and Children. This program is under the supervision of the State Committee of Ukraine for Family and Youth.
- In 2004, the government successfully dismantled 17 organized crime groups involved in trafficking cases.[12]
- In 2003, there was a review of 23 cases involving the trafficking of 330 Ukrainian women. In one case the traffickers sold 16 women to Italian and Spanish brothels in Hungary for US $800 apiece.
- In 2004, the government instructed all diplomatic officials abroad to identify Ukrainian trafficking victims and provide them with necessary travel documents.[13]
- The first case of trafficking charged under Article 124-1 was in Kamianets Podilskij. The person charged was a 25 year old former prostitute who said she realized she could earn more money as a trafficker than as a prostitute. Her modus operandi was to recruit women with the help of their

boyfriends. The second case involved the prosecution of three people accused of trafficking 200 women and girls (aged 13-25) from Ukraine to clubs in Greece, Turkey and Cyprus.

Laws and Prosecution

Moldovan legislation prohibits all types of trafficking and provides for severe penalties ranging from seven years to life imprisonment. In April 2002, a new criminal code was passed by the parliament. This legislation is still not in compliance with the internationally recognized definition of trafficking. However, in February 2005, the government drafted and sent to parliament new legislation to address all aspects for trafficking in a comprehensive manner. [14]

Moldova has made progress in its law enforcement efforts, but many suspect that the Ministry of Interior's Anti-Trafficking Unit limits its investigations in part because of pressure from high level officials who are complicit in trafficking. However, in 2004 the unit did open 274 investigations – nearly 100 more than in 2003 – and the courts convicted 16 persons for trafficking offenses including 7 for trafficking in children. Thirteen of those convicted received prison sentences of 2-16 years. [15]

In 1998, Ukraine updated its criminal law against trafficking in human beings, and in September 2001, the country passed legislation defining human trafficking as a criminal offense, along with pornography and sexual exploitation. In 2004, the government charged 138 persons with trafficking crimes, initiated 68 trafficking prosecutions, and courts convicted traffickers in 67 cases. Unfortunately, only 22 persons were sentenced to prison while the others were put on probation.

PROBLEMS

Official involvement and complicity in trafficking continued to be a problem and reports persist about high-level official intervention, which may result in significant sentence reductions. During 2004, the government did not investigate nor prosecute any cases of trafficking-related corruption. Authorities are now investigating a former Moldovan policeman for trafficking women to the U.A.E.. Judges are often corrupt and downgrade trafficking charges to pimping for lesser penalties.[16]

Police efforts at enforcing laws are hampered by a lack of clear mechanisms of enforcement, and the corruption of police by traffickers – victims often do not turn to the police for help, because they fear harassment, physical abuse, prosecution, and the loss of confidentiality. Police units sometimes known as the "moral police," units that are meant to be addressing these problems, are underfunded and lack critical supplies such as cars and communication technology.

The government of Moldova has not developed social programs for the prevention or rehabilitation of trafficking victims. Moldova also lacks data or sufficient information about internal trafficking and the local prostitution market. The situation in Ukraine is not much better than in Moldova.

Organized crime is strong in both Moldova and Ukraine and includes Albanian groups, and the Russian, Moldovan, and Ukrainian mafias. These criminal groups have started using air travel as a means of trafficking, something that was not done on a large scale prior to 2002. Trafficked women are traveling with legal documents, including Schengen visas, directly to Western Europe. Even though this travel is more expensive, it is more profitable for traffickers because it immediately burdens the women with huge indebtedness to the traffickers.

New trafficking channels are opening up especially to Russia for trafficking of children, elderly people, orphans and handicapped people, for begging and sexual exploitation.

Also, trafficking of women is increasing to Saudi Arabia, the United Arab Emirates, and Israel via Egypt. Many women are traveling to Turkey through the Ukraine (Odessa) and Bulgaria and although many of them are trafficked, there is little data collection concerning their requests for assistance.

According to the Center for the Prevention of Trafficking of Women (CPTW), trafficking from Moldova is not declining, but the phenomenon is becoming less apparent. NGOs report that the number of identified and assisted victims of trafficking from Moldova and Ukraine to the Balkan Countries decreased in 2003. However, there is evidence that new destination countries are replacing those in the Balkan region since trafficking to and from the Balkans has become more risky with new anti-trafficking actions and measures being put in place.

> *Recently, police in Kosovo, backed up by British and Norwegian peacekeeping troops, raided a bar near the capital Pristina, They found Serbians and Albanians - enemies in war time – now working together as pimps, trading in Moldovan women whose passports they held. Although the women were taken to safe houses, they had to be moved frequently to avoid pimps who were trailing them in order to get them back. This suggests that some of the local authorities in Kosovo were involved in the trafficking.[17]*

WORK BY NGOS AND INTERNATIONAL ORGANIZATIONS

IOM is working in Ukraine and Moldova on anti-trafficking campaigns. IOM and its respective networks of NGOs provide almost all of the direct and reintegration services to trafficked victims in Moldova. There are two shelters for victims of trafficking in Moldova in the capital city, Chisinau. One is managed by a local NGO, and the other by IOM. IOM also began managing a new shelter for trafficked minors in 2003.

The international NGO, La Strada, is also working in Ukraine and Moldova on anti-trafficking campaigns. Their work includes:

- raising public awareness by encouraging the media to publish and broadcast news stories on trafficking
- running an educational campaign by working with school teachers to educate children about trafficking issues (other NGOs are also running educational campaigns)
- interacting with law enforcement officials
- providing victim assistance, including a hotline service, emergency assistance, and long-term assistance with return and reintegration
- establishing relationships among government officials in various countries and using these connections to facilitate victim assistance and return.

Other NGOs are also running educational campaigns, and some Ukrainian NGOs have created hotlines for victim assistance: in Ukraine these NGOs include the Women for Women Centers in Lviv, Donetsk, Dnipropetrovsk, and the Donbas Women's Centre in Luhonsk.

Notes:

1. While the education itself is free, transportation, textbooks, heating, etc., are not.
2. *Ukraine Women's Work, Discrimination Against Women in the Ukrainian Labor Force,* Human Rights Watch Vol. 15 No. 4 (D), August 2003.
3. Information from the Moldovan Embassy in Russia.
4. These numbers are estimates from UNDP and IOM.
5. *Victims of Trafficking and Violence Protection Act of 2000: Trafficking in Persons Report,* (Washington, D.C., U.S. Department of State, 2005).
6. *Return &Reintegration Project, Situation Report,* IOM Kosovo, Feb. 2000 to April 2002.
7. Ibid.

8. *First Annual Report on Victims of Trafficking in South Eastern Europe,* The Stability Pact for South Eastern Europe, The Regional Clearing Point (RCP), 2003: 75-78.

9. *Sex Traffic: Trafficking of Women and Girls for Forced Prostitution,* Amnesty International UK, 2002. See: <http://www.amnesty.org.uk/sextraffic/>.

10. *Victims of Trafficking and Violence Protection Act of 2000: Trafficking in Persons Report,* 2005.

11. Ibid.

12. Ibid.

13. Ibid.

14. Ibid.

15. Ibid.

16. Ibid.

17. As told by an international worker in Kosovo, June 2005.

Conclusion

Trafficking in women and children for sexual exploitation is a worldwide problem which has reached unprecedented levels, but there is still limited action and little coordination on the part of governments, international agencies, and NGOs in responding to the phenomenon. Knowledge about the issue continues to be relatively weak and research has not moved much beyond mapping the problem, reviewing applicable legal frameworks, and proposing policy responses.

In spite of continuous involvement on the issue by the UN, the EU, the Council of Europe and some countries by creating international frameworks and encouraging states to support and implement them, the response of many governments has been minimal. Most states are still not able to provide reliable data on trafficking even within their borders or define the number of their citizens who are directly involved. Most cannot effectively differentiate between a victim of trafficking and an ordinary prostitute. Law enforcement as it pertains to trafficking remains inadequate both on a national and international level primarily because of the persistent general perception that trafficked women and children freely choose to migrate and allow themselves to be sold.

Much of this confusion arises out of the fact that the trade in human beings is an integral part of international labor migration and cannot be separated from it. Women and children are caught in the web of trafficking because they, as all migrants, are pushed to leave their own countries by their own or their families' desires for a better life and a way out of poverty, and simultaneously they are pulled abroad by the opportunity for gainful employment and a better life. But as legal migration becomes more restrictive, it becomes more difficult for them to succeed in fulfilling their desire to migrate, and they are then lured into the hands of traffickers who they often see as their only means of migrating on a regular or irregular way. Through this many end up in the nightmare of forced labor and sexual slavery.

Most of the data concerning trafficking and sexual slavery is limited to official statistics, which are based on short interviews with women who have either been deported or who have participated in return programs, that offer services only to those victims who meet specific criteria. Much of the information coming from these trafficking victims is incomplete because of the victims' lack of knowledge of the entire picture of the operation. Women and children who were trafficked are seldom able to provide precise data as to where they have been and who was involved. This is because they could not, as they were being trafficked, physically see what was going on, were not told anything, or what was told to them was false. Also, of course, victims' testimony is always affected by the fear of possible retribution from the traffickers both against them and their families, and also of the consequences they might face from local law enforcement if they tell the truth. In all of the data gathering, it is interesting to note that the role of organised crime and the increased demand for paid sex is rarely the focus, leaving these aspects to journalists and some NGOs who attempt to shed light on this dark side of the issue.

One fact revealed by testimony from nearly all victims is the role that difficult life circumstances, primarily poverty, play in a victim's decision to migrate. But poverty alone does not offer a full explanation for migration and trafficking of women and children. One must examine the situation at the local level to fully realize how women and children who desire to migrate fall into the trap of the traffickers and how a decision to migrate was made by the woman or child or by her family in order to improve the quality of life of those at home.

The limited choices of women and girls render them more vulnerable to trafficking and they are usually victimised in a number of ways. They can be deceived about the nature of the work they are undertaking; they may not be informed about the conditions under which they will have to work; they may not even know their final destination. Instead of going to Italy, they might end up in Bosnia and Herzegovina; instead of Germany, perhaps they will find themselves in Egypt on their way to Israel; instead of France, they end up in Mexico as the first stop on their way to their final destination in the United States. Traffickers may seize their documents or give them false ones. Victims may overstay their visas and work in irregular venues, risking arrest and detention. Their work may be unpaid or underpaid because of the debts to agents and employers. They are under constant pressure from the traffickers and their "owners" and this may lead them to seek relief through drugs.

These are known facts, and yet the governments of the countries of origin, destination and transit have made little progress in working alone or together to combat trafficking in women and children. Action has too often been directed at punishing the victims of trafficking rather than the traffickers. Immigration laws are written in a way to punish the victims and policies to provide social support for victims are still not well formulated nor put into practice. In spite of the adoption of National Action Plans and appointments of National Coordinators, countries of destination and origin, for the most part, have no clear policy and no coherent plan on trafficking, It is evident that the adoption of appropriate legislation as well as the adoption and implementation of international treaties concerning trafficking in women and children will take time.

Trafficking in human beings for the purpose of sexual exploitation is a reflection of the nature of the global market economy in which markets react immediately to current demand. Demand exists and supply follows to those places where demand is highest. And the fact that the goods are living, breathing, and feeling human beings, and not the product of a factory is a matter of indifference to the impersonal mechanisms of the market. This means that in order to effectively stem the tide of trafficking, aggressive pressure must be maintained by all levels of society: individual, local, state, regional, and international.

REGIONAL AND INTERNATIONAL POLICY MEASURES

At the European level both the European Union and the Council of Europe have taken a number of actions, communications and decisions regarding trafficking. The OSCE, the Stability Pact Trafficking in Human Beings Task Force (SPTTF)which closed in October 2004, and the Southern European Cooperative Initiative (SECI Centre) have undertaken significant capacity building in South Eastern Europe at the levels of governance, law enforcement, and the NGO sector. Many other organizations have made important contributions to combating trafficking. UN agencies, especially UNICEF, international organizations such as IOM, and international NGOs, especially La Strada and International Catholic Migration Commission (ICMC), have all done important work.

But what is still missing is an anti-trafficking system that can overcome the obstacles to effective implementation of action plans and relevant laws. The need for such successful interventions is already recognised. However, to devise such a system requires more than just research since in most countries or regions there are obvious similarities and differences in methods and approaches to the phenomenon of trafficking.

The approach of the United States Department of State which includes yearly monitoring has been a positive step. The system has increased awareness of the issue and forced its attention on countries that might otherwise not regard human trafficking as a priority. The State Department, through its Office to Monitor and Combat Trafficking in Persons, has established a set of minimum standards which must be satisfied in order to qualify countries for non-humanitarian aid. Countries are evaluated according to their efforts on:

1. Legal codes and law enforcement
2. Protection of and support for victims
3. Prevention efforts

Those which have complied with the basic standards are placed in "Tier 1." Those in "Tier 2" are regarded as having made significant efforts to comply, and those accorded "Tier 3" status are deemed not to have made sufficient efforts. Countries are evaluated every year based on the year's activities to combat trafficking. This classification has resulted in some controversy about the placement of some countries which indicates a need for additional measures that would compensate for the disparities in the resources and capacity of each state. Also, some countries have expressed concern with the process which they see as unfair since, in some cases, certain countries appear to receive preferred status.

Since common standards do not exist, there is a danger of imposing unrealistic and maybe irrelevant standards. On the other hand, there is a permanent need for restating human rights principals and for maintaining a focus on the rights and needs of trafficked women. A solution could be found in the creation of more opportunities for NGOs within Europe and at the same time more opportunities for regional cooperation on several levels.

The effect of globalization on the spread of human trafficking should be taken seriously, particularly in the economic area, and help in stimulating the economies of countries in transition could be an important step. Financial assistance from international organizations and wealthier countries should be considered for poor countries who cannot afford the judicial infrastructure necessary to tackle the problem. The aid should focus on training as well as establishing a system to adequately and regularly pay salaries to judges, police, and border guards,

NATIONAL ANTI-TRAFFICKING EFFORTS

Although the focus on this book has been the situation in the developing countries of Southeast Europe, all states that are countries of origin, transit, or destination must be actively involved at home in the fight against trafficking and sexual slavery. To focus efforts only on the countries of origin and transit, misses the point that the major markets for trafficked women and children are Western Europe, the United States, the Arab World, Israel, the Far East, and Mexico. If these destination countries do not take strong action against this scourge in their own states, it will be difficult, if not impossible, to stop trafficking of women and children.

Several studies have systematically examined trafficking for sexual exploitation through the perspective of best practices and obstacles to reaching objective results and statistics. These studies identified three major obstacles to effective action: corruption, inadequate resources, and lack of training including a failure to define a strategy to carry out relevant policies.

There is also considerable agreement among a number of experts on the primary barriers to effectively combating trafficking for the purpose of sexual exploitation. These include an inadequate legal base; ineffective law enforcement; lack of knowledge and specialization; lack of interest on the part of the authorities tasked with combating trafficking from the legal side; and the actual involvement of authorities in trafficking from the criminal side. Considering these factors, it is not surprising that legal reform has generally been limited and that little attention has been paid to the fact that traffickers easily evade prosecution.

It is critical that relevant national legislation includes the term "victim of trafficking," "sexual slavery," and "sexual exploitation." This will help ensure the principle that trafficked women and children are not criminalized, and that they have a fundamental right to protection, accommodation, and health services instead of being treated as criminals and deported. One recommended strategy emphasizes that laws relating to trafficking should be reviewed to make sure that they are effective in protecting trafficked women, especially when the women are involved in legal proceedings over a trafficking offence. But, unfortunately, even where new laws have been passed, their implementation has not proceeded constructively. One explanation for this has been that some judges do not understand the law.

Countries must also consider legislation that would help to curb the market for sex services from trafficked women and children by holding the client responsible and passing and implementing laws which would encourage clients to be significantly more discriminating. Clients should face the possibility of prosecution and punishment if they purchase the sexual services of a trafficked person.

Corruption of officials is widely recognized. In some cases this has included high government officials and judges. But most commonly it is with the border police who take money from traffickers for turning a blind eye to their activities, and the police who make procedural mistakes to undermine evidence. Little attention has been focused on the fact that often officials are underpaid or do not have the elementary material resources to enable them to perform their jobs properly. However, corruption generally persists because it is well tolerated. Until governments enforce anti bribery measures, including adequate punishment for officials accepting bribes, this problem will continue to frustrate efforts to curb trafficking.

There is a clear need for National Action Plans which address local realities and are based on an assessment of the current situation on the ground, including capabilities and priorities.

LOCAL KNOWLEDGE

Although trafficking is a global phenomenon, it has become even more crucial for those in the governmental and NGO sectors to understand the essential motivation and circumstances within which women and children found themselves when they were recruited. Also, it is necessary to understand the factors that make them vulnerable during recruiting as well as during the process of reintegration when they return to their countries of origin.

Lack of understanding of the local and individual contexts is leading us to be less effective in combating trafficking in human beings. It is essential for state governments to put more responsibilities on the local level including local governments, police, NGOs, and social service workers including providing more financial resources to develop and maintain effective programs to combat trafficking.

Changing from a global to a local approach entails using all available facilities from the local schools to the local cultural center as tools for raising awareness. There should also be more effort put into monitoring the community. Police who are familiar to citizens can be more helpful in collecting information then state agencies with only bureaucratic connection to the local level.

For instance, we currently know very little about the structure of trafficking networks - both those that are highly organised and those that are not. The information we do have is leading us to the conclusion that everything starts from the local level as individual initiatives or initiatives of organized crime which might, for example, use women who are former victims of trafficking as recruiters. This is one more reason to invest in programs that support victims of trafficking and help them rebuild their lives in a way that helps them refute all connections with organizations involved in trafficking.

In fact, good practices on the local level could finally destroy this dispersed chain of traffickers. If this approach were applied globally, it would have a direct impact on trafficking between countries. An investment on the local level would in the long run save money now being spent on shelters and advocacy programs.

INDIVIDUAL ACTION

If there were no customers for the sex services of women and children, there would be no trafficking. Therefore, responsibility for this phenomenon must also be borne by the customer. Individuals in the community must inform themselves about trafficking, that it results in sexual slavery, and vocally condemn any association with this practice.

Individuals can support victims of trafficking as they attempt to reintegrate into their communities rather than labeling them as prostitutes. Individuals can also support the work of NGOs and of their communities as they educate people about the dangers of irregular migration and refuse to expose themselves and their family members to the possibility of trafficking.

You may personally help the fight against trafficking in human beings by offering your support to one of the organizations listed in the back of this book. If you know of a person who is a victim of trafficking or in danger of being trafficked, contact an organization hotline, the police, and the embassy of the victim's country of origin.

CORRUPTION INHIBITS PROGRESS ON TRAFFICKING

Government corruption is a major impediment in the fight against trafficking for many countries. The scale of government corruption relating to trafficking in persons can range from localized to endemic. Countries facing such official corruption need to develop effective tools with which to tackle the problem. Some anti-corruption practices that have been effectively used by Central and Eastern European countries to bolster the fight against human trafficking include: performing psychological testing of law enforcement officers, including tests for stability, intelligence, character, ethics, and loyalty; requiring mandatory ethics briefings; issuing standard identification badges; conducting random integrity tests; distributing and using best practices manuals; randomly checking officials' personal belongings and cash; publicizing anonymous anti-corruption hotlines; rotating personnel, particularly at high volume border checkpoints; increasing wages; giving performance incentive awards; providing training to help personnel to better understand the importance of their work; requiring an oath of service; and, instituting routine administrative checks, for example of immigration records.

U.S. Department of State, Trafficking in Persons Report June 14, 2004

List of Abbreviations And Acronyms

CoE	Council of Europe
COM	Committee of Ministers of the CoE
EU	European Union
EUPM	European Union Police Mission
FBiH	Federation of Bosnia and Herzegovina
FRY	Federal Republic of Yugoslavia
FYR Macedonia	Former Yugoslave Republic of Macedonia
ICMC	International Catholic Migration Committee
IGO	Inter-Governmental Organization
IHRLG	International Human Rights Law Group
ILO	International Labour Organization
IOM	International Organization for Migration
IPTF	International Police Task Force
KFOR	Kosovo Force
KM	Convertible Mark (currency of BiH)
NATO	North Atlantic Treaty Organization
NGO	Non-governmental organization
NPA	National Plan of Action
ODIHR	OSCE Office for Democratic Institutions and Human Rights
OSCE	Organization for Security and Cooperation in Europe
RCP	Regional Clearing Point
RS	Republika Srpska
SBS	State Border Service

SECI	Southern European Cooperative Initiative
SEE	South Eastern Europe
SFOR	Stabilization Force of the Partnership for Peace
SIMPOC	Statistical Information and Monitoring Programme on Child Labour
SPTTF	Stability Pact Task Force on Trafficking in Human Beings
STOP	Special Trafficking Operations Programme
TIP Report	U.S. Department of StateTrafficking in Persons Report
TPIU	Trafficking and Prostitution Investigative Unit
UMCOR	United Methodist Committee on Relief
UN	United Nations
UNDP	United Nations Development Programme
UNHCR	United Nations High Commissioner for Refugees
UNOHCHR	United Nations Office of the High Commissioner for Human Rights
UNICEF	United Nations Children's Fund
UNMIBH	United Nations Mission in Bosnia and Herzegovina

NGOS and International Organizations Combating Trafficking in Human Beings

Southeast and East Europe

Albania

Counseling Center for Women and Girls, Tirana
qkgv@albnet.net

The Hearth, Vlora
Qvatra@icc-al.org
QPS-Vatra@aul.sanx.net

Bosnia and Herzegovina

Association "Zena BiH"
Telephone: + 387 36 550-339
zenabih@cob.net.ba
www.zenabih.ba

LARA, Bijeljina
lara@rstel.net

IHRLG-International Human Rights Law Group
Sarajevo
ihrlgbih@open-net.ba
www.hrlawgroup.org

La Strada Bosnia Herzegovina, Mostar
Telephone/fax 00 387 36 557 191/192
lastrada@cob.net.ba
http://www.cob.net.ba/lastrada

Bulgaria

> La Strada Bulgaria
> Animus Association
> Telephone 00 359 2 981 6740, 00 359 2 987 3198
> animus@mbox.cit.bg
> Animus@animusassociation.org

Croatia

> International Catholic Migration Commission / ICMC
> Zagreb
> Croatia@ICMC.net
>
> Women's Room, Zagreb
> zenska.soba@zamir.net

Macedonia

> 'Open Gate' Women's Lobby
> and Action against Violenceand Trafficking
> in Persons/La Strada Macedonia
> Telephone 00 389 2 700 107
> Fax 00 389 2 700 367
> E-mail lastrada@on.net.mk
> Hotline: 02 2777 070
> sosline@lastrada.org.mk

Moldova

> La Strada, Chisinau
> Hotline: 0 800 77777
> Hotline (international calls): 373 22233309
> lsmoldova@ls.moldline.net

Romania

> Strada Campineanu
> Bloc 2, Scara C, Etaj 3, Apt. 20
> Judet Arges - 0300
> Pitesti, Romania
> 00 40 48 630 843 or 627 916
> reachingoutrom@yahoo.com

State Union of Serbia and Montenegro including Kosovo

> Antitrafficking Center Belgrade
> act@beotel.yu
> antitraffickingcenter@yahoo.com

> ASTRA a network of NGO's for anti-
> sex trafficking action Belgrade
> astranet@sezampro.yu
> www.astra.vds.org.yu

> Women's Safety House Podgorica, Montenegro
> shelter@cg.yu

> UMCOR, Women's Program, Kosovo
> kizid@hotmail.com

Ukraine

> La Strada - Ukraine
> PO Box 246
> 01030 Kyiv Ukraine
> Tel/Fax: (380-44) 224-04-46
> Hotline: +38 (044) 224-0446
> lastrada@ukrpack.net

European Union

Belgium

> Mouvement du Nid ASBL
> 14 rue Hydrauliqu
> B-1210 Bruxelles
> Tel: (0032)2 217 84 72, Fax: (0032) 2 217 60 16

France

> Les delegations du Mouvement du Nid:
>
> 31 avenue Clemenceau
> 61800 Mulhouse
> Tel:(0033) 3 89 56 63 25, Fax:(0033) 3 89 56 63 25,
> Email: lenid.mulhouse@wanadoo.fr
>
> 1 quai Saint-Jean
> 67000 Strasbourg
> Tel:(0033) 3 88 32 77 67, Fax:(0033) 3 88 32 77 67
> Email: mouvement.du.nid67@wanadoo.fr
>
> Secretariat Regional
> 8 avenue Gambetta/75 020 Paris
> Tel:(0033) 1 42 82 17 00
>
> 7 place de Lavalette
> 38028 Grenoble Cedex 1
> Tel:(0033) 4 76 90 16 62
> Email: nidgre@free.fr

2 rue de la Loubiere
13006 Marseille
Tel:(0033) 4 91 92 04 84
Email: nidmarseille@free.fr

7 place des Terreaux BP 1003
69201 Lyon Cedex 01
Tel:(0033) 4 78 30 12 84

Femmes de l'Est
femmesdelest@yahoo.com

Germany

Ban Ying Koordinationsstelle
Anklamerstr. 38
10115 Berlin
Tel.: 030 440 63 73 /74
Ban-Ying@ipn.de

KOK - Federal Association Against Traffic in
Women and Violence Against Women in the
Migration Process
BehlerstratBe 35
14467 Potsdam
Tel: 03-31-28-03-30-0/5
Fax: 03-31-28-03-30/7
kok.potsdam@t-online.de

Netherlands

Fundación Esperanza
Postbus 920788
1090 AB
Amsterdam Holland
Tel: 31-20-4686934
esperanza@wxs.nl

STV Foundation
Against Trafficking in Women
P.O. Box 1455
Utrecht 3500-BL

The Netherlands
P: 31-30-271-6044
Fax: 31-30-271-6084
stv@stv.nl

Slovenia

"KLJUC", Ljubljana
Kljuc center@hotmail.com

Association Against Sexual Abuse
Zpsz@email.sl

Spain

Project ESPERANZA
Congregation of the Adoratrices
Religious Community
Apartado Postal 50905 AP (P.O. Box)
28080 Madrid Espana
Tel: 34-913860643
Fax: 34-913732141
esperanza@globalnet.es

United Kingdom

Amnesty International
99-119 Rosebery Avenue
London EC1R 4RE United Kindgon
Tel: +44-207-814-6200
Fax: +44-207-833-1510
info@amnesty.org.uk

Anti-Slavery International
Thomas Clarkson House
The Stableyard
Broomgrove Road
London SW9 9TL UK
Tel: +44 (0)20 7501 8920
Fax: +44 (0)20 7738 4110
antislavery@antislavery.org

United States of America

Trafficking Information and Referral
Hotline 1 888 373 7888

Coalition to Abolish Slavery and Trafficking
Little Tokyo Service Center
231 E. 3rd St., Suite G104
Los Angeles, California 90013
Tel:(213) 473-1611; Fax: (213) 473-1601
cast@trafficked-women.org

Free the Slaves
1755 Massachusetts Ave., NW
Washington DC, 20036
Tel: 1 202 244 18651
Tel: 866-324-FREE

International Human Rights Law Group
Initiative Against Trafficking in Persons
1200 - 18th Street NW
Washington, DC 20036
Tel: 202-822-4600, ext. 27Fax: 202-822-4606
trafficking@hrlawgroup.org

Human Rights Watch
350 Fifth Ave. 34th Floor
New York, New York 10118
Tel: 212 290 4700
www.hrw.org

Stop Human Traffic
www.stophumantraffic.org

International Organizations

IOM (International Organization for Migration)
www.iom.int
Offices located throughout Southeast Europe

OSCE-ODIHR
Area Office for the Balkans
00-557 Warsaw, Poland
Tel: 48 22 520 0600
www.osce.org/odihr

SECI Center
Romania, 050711 Bucharest, no. 3-5, Calea 13
Septembrie, sector 5
Tel: (+4021) 303.60.09

UNICEF
Ujazdowskie 19
Svetozara markovica 58
Belgrade, Serbia and Montenegro
Tel: 381 11 3602 100
www.unicef.org

UNOHCHR
Sarajevo, Bosnia and Herzegovina
Tel: 387 33 276 860
www.unhchr.ch

References

Annual Trafficking in Persons Report. U.S. Department of
State, Office to Monitor and Combat Trafficking in Persons,
Washington, D.C. 2001, 2002, 2003, 2004, 2005. See: <http://
www.state.gov/g/tip/>

Dordevic, J. and Dekic, S. *Trgovina zenama, prirucnik za
novinare* (Trafficking in Women, A Guide for Journalists),
Belgrade: Anti-Sex Trafficking Action, 2003.

Baumann, Z. "From Pilgrim to Tourist-or A Short History
of Identity." In *Cultural Identity* edited by Hall and du Gay.
London: Sage Press, 1996.

Black,M. *The No-Nonsense Guide to International
Development*. London: New Internationalist™ Publications
Ltd, 2002.

Bokhorst, H. *Femmes dans les griffes des aigles : Les filières
de la prostitution albanaise*. Brussels: Editions Labor, 2003.

Boullanger, H. *La criminalité économique en Europe*. Paris :
Presses universitaires de France, 2002

Brown, Louise. *Sex Slaves, The Trafficking of Women in Asia*.
London: Virago Press, 2001.

Child Sexual Abuse in Europe. Compiled by May-Chahal, C.
and Herczog, M. Strasbourg: Council of Europe Publishing
2003.

Crawford, A. *The Local Governance of Crime*. New York: Oxford University Press, 1999.

Cretin, T. *Mafias du monde: Organisations criminelles transnationales. Actualités et Perspectives*. Paris :Presses Universitaires de France, 2002.

Dupont-Monod, C. *Histoire d'une prostituée*. Paris : Bernard Grasset, 2003.

Dusch, S. *Le trafic d'êtres humains*. Paris : Presses Universitaires de France, 2002.

End Child Exploitation, Faces of Exploitation. UNICEF, 2003.

First Annual Report on Victims of Trafficking in South Eastern Europe. Stability Task Force on Trafficking in Human Beings, Regional Clearing Point (RCP), 2003.

Fondation Scelles. *La prostitution adulte en Europe*. Ramonville Saint-Agne : Editions érès, 2002.

Gaon, Igor Davor. *Reflection Tables on Immigration and Human Rights : Trafficking in Human Beings*. Office of the Commissioner for Human Rights, Athens: Council of Europe, 2003.

Gaon, Igor Davor. "Trafficking in Human Beings – Violation of Human Rights," in *Human Rights and Immigration*. Strasbourg: Council of Europe, 2003.

Gaon, Igor Davor. *Combating Trafficking of Children in Europe: Trafficking and Exploitation of Adolescents and Minors*. Strasbourg: Council of Europe, 2004

Gaon, Igor Davor. *Trafficking in Human Beings, Bulgaria.* Prepared for the Bulgarian School of Politics. Strasbourg: Council of Europe, 2004.

Gaon, Igor Davor. *Trafficking in Human Beings, Moldova.* Prepared for the European Institute for Political Studies Moldova. Strasbourg: Council of Europe, 2004.

Geddes, A. *The Politics of Migration and Immigration in Europe.* London: Sage Publications, 2003.

Hopes Betrayed. Vol. 14, NO. 9 (D). New York: Human Rights Watch, 2002.

Human Rights Report on Trafficking of Persons, Especially Women and Children. Washington, D.C.: The Protection Project, 2002.

Landesman, Peter. "The Girls Next Door." *New York Times Magazine*, January 25, 2004.

Ligardimier, C. *La Prostitution.* Toulouse : Les Essentiels 1999.

Limanowska, Barbara. *Trafficking in Human Beings in South Eastern Europe.* Belgrade :UNICEF, UNOHCHR, OSCE/ ODIHR, 2002.

Limanowska, Barbara. *Trafficking in Human Beings in South Eastern Europe.* Belgrade :UNICEF, UNOHCHR, OSCE/ ODIHR, 2003.

Malarek, V. *The Natashas: The New Global Sex Ttrade.* Toronto: Penguin Group, 2003.

Migration and Refugee Policies: An Overview. Edited by Bernstein, A. and Weiner, M. New York: Continuum, 1999.

New Challenges for Migration Policy in Central and Eastern Europe. Prepared by the International Organisation for Migration and International Center for Migration Policy Development. The Hague: T. M. C. Asser Press, 2002.

Nor, M. *La Prostitution.* Paris: Le Cavalier Bleu Editions, 2001.

Patterson, O. *Population in an Interacting World.* Ed. W. Alonso. Cambridge: Harvard University Press, 1987.

Pearson, E. *Human traffic, Human Rights: Redefining Victim Protection.* London: Anti-Slavery International, 2002.

Preventing Violence Against Women: A European Perspective. Strasbourg: Council of Europe Publishing, 2003.

Research on Child Trafficking in Bosnia and Herzegovina. Sarajevo: UNICEF and Save the Children Norway, 2005.

Ruggiero, V. *Crime and Markets: Essays in Anti-Criminalogy.* Oxford: Oxford University Press, 2001.

Seabrook, J. *Travels in the Skin Trade.* Chicago, Pluto Press, 1996.

Seabrook, J. *Children of Other Worlds: Exploitation in the Global Market.* London: Pluto Press, 2001.

Skrobanek, S. et al. *The Traffic in Women: Human Realities of the International Sex Trade.* New York: Zed Books Ltd, 1997.

Stulhofer, Alexandar et al. *Trafficking in Women and Children for Sexual Exploitation*. Zagreb: Center for Transition and Civil Society Research, International Organization for Migration, 2002.

The Political Economy of New Slavery. Edited by Van den Anker. New York: C. Palgrave Macmillan, 2004.

Transnational Prostitution: Changing Patterns in a Global Context. Edited by Thorbek, S. and Pattanaik, B. New York: Zed Books Ltd, 2002.

Urban Crime Prevention; A Guide for Local Authorities. Strasbourg: Council of Europe Publishing, 2002.

Woodward, A.E. *Going for Gender Balance*. Strasbourg: Council of Europe Publishing, Strasbourg, 2002.

Map Reference
The World Fact Book. Reference Maps. Central Intelligence Agency Website: <www.cia.gov>.

Printed in the United States
105194LV00003B/7/A